EARLY 20TH CENTURY UFOS
AMERICAN SIGHTINGS
1900-1919

By Noe Torres & John LeMay

ROSWELL BOOKS.COM
Roswell, New Mexico · Edinburg, Texas

© COPYRIGHT 2021 Noe Torres & John LeMay
All rights reserved.

Cover Illustration by Jolyon Yates

Torres, Noe.
LeMay, John.
 Early 20th Century UFOs:
 American Sightings (1900-1919)
  1. History—Early 20th Century. 2. Ufology—Study of Unidentified Flying Objects. 3. Folklore, early day America.

The "Thing" Found in the Ice

My Esquimaux informants state that for nearly an hour after its release the creature lay like a mummy. Then, as night fell, the eyelids quivered, and rheum was seen to issue from them. All the while Mr. Sirk was engaged in massaging the "thing's" wrists and heart. With the coming dusk animation stirred its body. The lips trembled, the fingers shook nervously.

Suddenly as the moon rose, the tongue protruded and articulation was heard. Mr. Sirk fell over in a faint and all his servants, save three, fled. The remaining servants tenderly put their master, who for two days had neglected to take food, upon a dog-sled and bore him with the strange acquisition to this home. Recovering, Mr. Sirk saw again the weird being and found it wholly alive and seated on a chair like any human creature, dispatching with gluttonous haste all the visible eatables on the servant's table; its first food for possibly 4,000 years.

My Esquimaux messengers added that when daylight came the creature acted as one dead, and remained so until nightfall, when it emerged from its coma, and, bearing itself like a high-caste human, uttered strange speech and made overt attempts to convey its thoughts.

My next letter will be written from personal observation, as it is no longer possible to endure conjecture. I leave for the Sirk estate tonight and will advise you of developments.

Newspaper Article on Otherworldly Transmissions c.1900

Noe Torres: For my mom, Maria de Jesus, an avid reader who encouraged me to read and write at a very young age - and who sparked my interest in UFOs by telling me of a strange encounter she had in the 1940s.

John LeMay: For my good friend Dr. John Stamey, keep on believing!

ACKNOWLEDGMENTS

This book, and the others in this series, would never have been written without the encouragement and support of a long list of dear friends, not the least of which is Ruben J. Uriarte, fellow traveler on our amazing interstellar flight.

PREFACE

BY THE YEAR 1900, the period that had encapsulated what we called "The Real Cowboys and Aliens" series in our previous three books was over. Vestiges of the Old West still clung to society until about 1915, when technological advancements caused "the old ways" of life to rapidly dissolve. For example, in the world of transportation, the horse and buggy quickly gave way to the "horseless carriage," i.e. the automobile. Generally, if people of the early 1900s could afford an automobile, they purchased one. Otherwise, they found themselves back in the saddle again, literally, at least for a while longer. Beginning in 1913, America's first truly affordable automobile, the Ford Motor Company's "Model T," finally sounded the death knell on horse-powered transportation. The automobile would slowly outpace the horse, with 15 million Model Ts rolling off Ford's assembly lines between 1913 and 1927.

Santos Dumont's Flight Around the Eiffel Tower
c.1901

The days of having to transport messages between physically distant point by horse, train, or boat were also becoming a relic of the past by the early 1900s, thanks to the telegraph and the telephone. Though invented by Alexander Graham Bell in 1885, telephones did not gain wide acceptance and usage in American homes until the early 1900s. The network infrastructure, which prefigured our modern Internet, eventually became robust enough that in 1904, three million phones were in use in America.

But the technological innovation that probably most impacted America – and the world – after 1900, was manned flight, which is important in relation to the topic of this book. As pointed out in our *Real Cowboys and Aliens* series, prior to the end of the 19th century, human beings had not taken to the air in any significant manner other than via non-steerable hot-air balloons that generally went straight up and came straight back down.

Although the first true airships, also called blimps or dirigibles, did not begin appearing in earnest until after 1900, our *Real Cowboys and Aliens* books disclosed hundreds and possibly thousands of sightings of "mysterious airships" throughout the United States beginning as early as the mid-1800s. It is suspected that some of these craft seen were early prototypes of the dirigibles that became more widespread after 1900, but not all of them. Many of these mysterious craft defied the technology of the time and could not have possibly been ordinary airships.

Before 1900, it was extremely rare to see a human being soaring overhead in any type of craft. This changed on December 17, 1903 when Orville and Wilbur Wright successfully flew humanity's first heavier-than-air aircraft. After this milestone, manned flight grew in leaps and bounds, with the first passenger airline starting up in 1914 and becoming much more common in the 1920s.

This Page: The Wright Brothers Famous Flight on December 17, 1903. Opposite: Early Day Glider.

Thus, we begin this new series of books with UFO stories from an age when ground-based observers were witnessing more and more airplanes and dirigibles. Even so, they also witnessed other craft that clearly did not square with the aviation technology of their time period.

Despite the growing number of legitimate aircraft, observers frequently still saw many unexplainable things in the sky. Among the stories we reveal in this book, National Guard soldiers at a camp in Pueblo, Colorado, saw glowing vehicles flying overhead with amazing speed and maneuverability. As in many other sightings from the early 1900s, these strange craft exhibited aviation technology that far surpassed man's abilities at the time.

In another remarkable story from this book, survivors of the 1912 sinking of the *RMS Titanic* saw strangely illuminated objects hovering along the horizon, as if observing what had happened. One survivor, watching these objects from a lifeboat, said they appeared to exhibit intelligence.

Also stunning is the story that at least one leading scientist of this era, Thomas Alva Edison, believed that the worldwide flu pandemic that killed an estimated 500 million people, might have come from outer space.

It's amazing to read these stories and come face-to-face with bizarre, unexplained historical incidents that are not commonly known. We know that UFOs have been with us since mankind's early history, and the early 20th century is certainly no exception, as our readers are about to discover

CONTENTS
ACKNOWLEDGMENTS vi
PREFACE vii

CHAPTERS

1.	The Horseshoe UFO	15
2.	Messages from Outer Space	21
3.	Celestial Starfish	29
4.	The Van Meter Visitors	33
5.	The Thing in the Mine	41
6.	Navy Ship Encounters UFOs	47
7.	The First Philadelphia Experiment	53
8.	The "Thing" Frozen in Ice	59
9.	"Mystery Meteor" in New York	67
10.	The Man Who Visited Mars	73
11.	The Airship Wave of 1906	83
12.	Music of the Airships	89
13.	UFO Explosion in Vermont	101
14.	All Hallows Eve Airship	107
15.	Airship Over the Salton Sea	113
16.	Attack of the Pigeon People	119
17.	The Abduction of Idella Ford	127
18.	UFOs Over the Titanic	137
19.	UFO Casts Shadow in Texas	145
20.	Little Green Man of Texas	151
21.	Hundreds See Fast Moving UFO	159
22.	Prospectors Encounter UFO	163
23.	Alien Music	173
24.	Mysterious Low Flying UFO	179
25.	UFO Over Lake Superior	183
26.	Multiple UFOs Over Colorado	191
27.	Close Encounter in Pennsylvania	197
28.	Texas Soldiers See UFO	201
POSTSCRIPT Virus from Outer Space?		205

INDEX 211
ABOUT THE AUTHORS 213

THE HORSESHOE UFO
October 1, 1900
Wilmington, Vermont

IN HIS BOOK *Unnatural Phenomena: A Guide to the Bizarre Wonders of North America,* Jerome Clark tells the amazing story of a "horseshoe" shaped UFO seen at several spots in Vermont in the Fall of 1900. Drawing from a number of local newspaper articles, a very unusual tale arises. At midnight on Monday, October 1, 1900, James Dinwiddle and George Buckley "saw a bright light on Mt. Pleasant [near Woodford, Vermont] that cannot be accounted for to date." The strange light would travel up and down and then "contour around in a circle several rods" [1 rod = 16.5 feet] before it came back to the place where it started.

EARLY 20th CENTURY UFOs

Considerable curiosity has been awakened to know what the bright light was that James Dinwiddle and George Buckley saw on the summit of Mount Pleasant last week Monday night at midnight. says a Woodford correspondent. The light would move up and down, going a considerable ways upward, and then make a contour on all sides and come back to the place of beginning. A surprising coincidence is, that at one o'clock in the morning of the same night, John Rooney was awake and happened to look out the window and on the summit of Haystack mountain he saw a bright light. The light acted queerly. It would go heavens high—thousands of feet—then come down and diverge off on either side, apparently a few rods, then go back to the place of beginning and go up again. Mr. Rooney called up his family and hired men, who witnessed the phenomenon with him until four o'clock in the morning, when the light seemed to go right down into the village of Wilmington and was not seen again.

Springfield (VT) Reporter, October 12, 1900, page 1

AMERICAN SIGHTINGS: 1900-1919

That same evening, at one o'clock in the morning John Rooney got an even better look at the strange craft flying over Haystack Mountain, about 13 miles away, near Wilmington, Vermont. The object caught Rooney's interest enough to where he thought it would be worth waking up his family and hired men to come watch it too. "The bright light acted queerly," Rooney said.

An article in the *Springfield (Vermont) Reporter* said, "The light would go heavens high – thousands of feet – then come down and diverge off on either side, apparently a few rods, then go back to the place of beginning and go up again."

"Mr. Rooney called up his family and hired men, who witnessed the phenomenon with him until four o'clock in the morning, when the light seemed to go right down into the village of Wilmington and was not seen again," the *Springfield Reporter* noted.

*1898 Photo of the Haystack Mountain Area
(NYPL Public Domain)*

EARLY 20th CENTURY UFOs

Something very interesting about the Haystack Mountain sighting is that it went on for three hours, which is an unusually long time for these sorts of events. The up-down and left-right maneuverability of the object is the same type of non-ballistic motion that has been observed in many other UFO sightings over the decades. Despite the early date of this incident (1900), remarkably it shares many characteristics with modern UFO sightings, in terms of the craft's motion and general appearance.

One local newspaper humorously concluded, "There are various opinions about the lights on the two mountains ten or a dozen miles apart on the same night. Local 'philosophers' are 'probing the matter,' and it is possible that outside lore will be required to fathom the mystery. We do not care to render any verdict this week."

And then there was another sighting a few days later, at 10 o'clock in the evening. This time the witnesses, the family of F. A. Gleason of nearby Woodford, Vermont, were able to get a clearer description of the craft. It was about ten feet in diameter, yellowish white in color and in the shape of a horseshoe but with "arms protruding from the inside." The family observed it fly only a few feet off the ground before it flew off over "Charles Sawyers into the mountain beyond." The article concluded by stating that, "If these strange lights have been seen in other towns we would like to know."

Interestingly, horseshoe-shaped UFOs have been seen in the skies many times over recent decades, including a rather dramatic sighting that

AMERICAN SIGHTINGS: 1900-1919

occurred in Cincinnati, Ohio, on January 31, 2019. It is certainly possible that these craft are not shaped like a horseshoe, but rather have an assembly of lights that gives the appearance of a horseshoe. The ship itself may be circular or some other shape. Since most of these sightings have occurred at nighttime, the actual shape of the vehicle is difficult to judge.

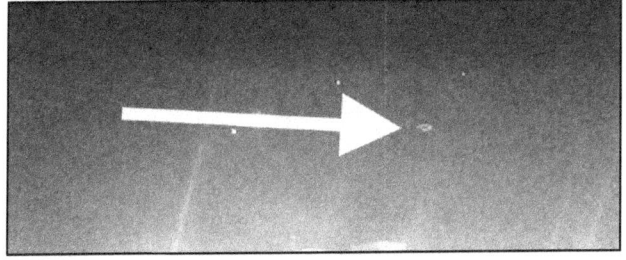

Horseshoe-shaped UFO photographed over Cincinnati, Ohio on 1-31-2019 (uforeport.co.uk)

EARLY 20th CENTURY UFOs

Nikola Tesla

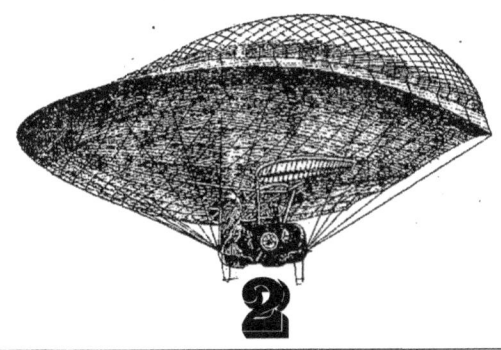

MESSAGES FROM OUTER SPACE

December 24, 1900
New York, New York

IN A SPECIAL Christmas Eve message in 1900, one of America's greatest scientists, engineers, and inventors, Nikola Tesla, expressed his conviction that he had received messages from intelligent beings on other planets. The story that Tesla could be receiving communications from extraterrestrials made headlines throughout the world, heralded as "a wonderful possibility."

In the *Gazette* of Cedar Rapids, Iowa, Tesla is quoted as saying, "In some experiments I have been conducting for some time, I have been noticing disturbances that have had a peculiar effect on my instruments."

EARLY 20th CENTURY UFOs

SIGNALS FROM THE STARS

Tesla Says His Instruments Are Vibrating with Messages Flashed across Space from Neighboring Worlds ---A Wonderful Possibility.

New York, Jan. 1--Nikola Tesla, the wizard of electricity, is completely satisfied that attempts are being made by the inhabitants of some other planet to communicate with the people of this earth.

"In some experiments I have been conducting for some time," said Mr. Tesla, "I have been noticing disturbances that have had a peculiar effect on my instruments. What these disturbances are caused by I am unable to say at present, but I am firmly convinced that they are the results of an attempt by some human beings, not of our world, to speak to us by signals.

"I am certain of some points in connection with these things I have noticed. I am absolutely certain that they are not caused by anything terrestrial. I know, too, that they are not caused by the sun or moon, and hence I am forced to the belief that they come from some other planet.

A Fascinating Problem.

"Aside from all that I have noticed and the question of probabilities, the question of interplanetary communication is one of the most fascinating that man can imagine. Since the conviction came to me that possibly we are on the eve of the most marvelous thing that has ever come to pass, I have been completely carried away by thinking of the wonderful possibilities that lie behind such a consummation.

"To begin with, supposing it were definitely discovered, as I feel certain that it will be, that the people of another planet were signaling to us, there would be the preliminary calls and their answers. These might take years to perfect. That is what I refer to in the 'One, Two, Three' of my message.

The Gazette (Cedar Rapids, Iowa), Jan. 1, 1901, p. 9

"What these disturbances are caused by, I am unable to say at present, but I am firmly convinced that they are the results of an attempt by some human beings, not of our world to speak to us by signals," Tesla said.

"I am certain of some points in connection with these things I have noticed. I am absolutely certain they are not caused by anything terrestrial. I know, too, that they are not caused by the sun or moon, and hence I am forced to the belief that they come from some other planet."

An avowed believer in life on other worlds, Tesla said, "Man on Earth is not the only being in God's great system of worlds that is in possession of a mind. Aside from all that I have noticed and the

AMERICAN SIGHTINGS: 1900-1919

question of probabilities, the question of interplanetary communication is one of the most fascinating that man can imagine. Since the conviction came to me that possibly we are on the eve of the most marvelous thing that has ever come to pass, I have been completely carried away by thinking of the wonderful possibilities that lie behind such a consummation."

Tesla explained that once communication was firmly set up, it would take a while for the two worlds to establish a "common basis of mutual understanding." When that was completed, "then would come such revelations as would astound us all," Tesla said, "Why, even as I ponder on the possibilities of all that lies in this marvel, I feel uplifted and almost, I might say, purified with even the contemplation of such a stupendous matter."

When pressed as to which of the planets in our solar system might be trying to contact Earth, Tesla's best guess was Venus. "I have noticed these disturbances when Venus is rising," he said, "and hence have come to the belief that perhaps while others have been planning to talk to Mars, Venus has been trying to signal to us."

As to what technology was being used to transmit messages to Earth, Tesla said, "Of course, the inhabitants of some other planet may be in possession of some power of which we know nothing, or they may have a greater control over electrical forces than we have. But it is reasonable to suppose that the signals I have noticed are electrical in their nature. In fact, they must be or my instruments would not have noticed them."

EARLY 20th CENTURY UFOs

Tesla closed his Christmas Eve message of 1900 by appealing to the world's scientists to set up "observatory stations" in a concerted effort to capture the interplanetary messages and to possibly answer them. He saw this development as critical to scientific exploration.

Tesla's Laboratory at Colorado Springs in 1899

AMERICAN SIGHTINGS: 1900-1919

Tesla's efforts to communicate with other planets was later profiled in the *Richmond (Virginia) Times*, which stated, "As he sat beside his instrument on the hillside in Colorado, in the deep silence of that austere, inspiring region, where you plant your feet in gold and your head brushes the constellations -- as he sat there one evening, alone, his attention, exquisitely alive at that juncture, was arrested by a faint sound from the receiver -- three fairy taps, one after the other, at a fixed interval. What man who has ever lived on this earth would not envy Tesla that moment!"

"Never before since the globe first swung into form had that sound been heard. Those three soft impulses, reflected from the sensitive disc of the receiver, had not proceeded from any Earthly source. The force which propelled them. The measure which regarded them, the significance they were meant to convey, had their origin in no mind native to this planet."

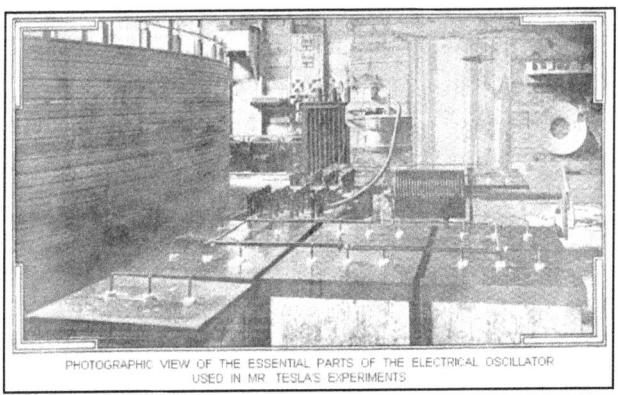

PHOTOGRAPHIC VIEW OF THE ESSENTIAL PARTS OF THE ELECTRICAL OSCILLATOR USED IN MR. TESLA'S EXPERIMENTS

From Collier's Weekly Magazine, Feb. 9, 1901, p. 5

EARLY 20th CENTURY UFOs

"They were sent, those marvelous signals, by a human being living and thinking so far away from us, both in space and in condition, that we can only accept him as a fact, not comprehend him as a phenomenon. Traveling with the speed of light, they must have been dispatched but a few moments before Tesla, in Colorado, received them. But they came from some Tesla on the planet Mars!"

His attempts to communicate with other planets were featured in the February 9, 1901 edition of *Collier's Weekly* Magazine, in which Tesla said, "At the present stage of progress, there would be no insurmountable obstacle in constructing a machine capable of conveying a message to Mars, nor would there be any great difficulty in recording signals transmitted to us by the inhabitants of that planet, if they be skilled electricians.... What a tremendous stir this would make in the world! How soon will it come? For that it will some time be accomplished must be clear to every thoughtful being. Something, at least, science has gained. But I hope that it will also be demonstrated soon that in my experiments in the West I was not merely beholding a vision but had caught sight of a great and profound truth."

To this day, the origin of the mystery sounds that Tesla received is still unknown. Some historians have suggested that he was picking up signals sent by Guglielmo Marconi from Italy or one of the other European inventors that were experimenting with wireless transmission of signals.

AMERICAN SIGHTINGS: 1900-1919

New York Herald, January 25, 1920, p. 71

Interestingly, Marconi himself, several years later, became convinced that he was receiving radio signals from the planet Mars. In a *New York Herald* article on January 25, 1920, Marconi is quoted as saying, "During my experiments with wireless, I have encountered many striking phenomena. I have received signals which quite conceivably might have arisen somewhere in interplanetary space."

When pressed as to whether the signals might be from other planets, Marconi replied, "Yes, the idea of interplanetary communication appears to me to be by no means outside the range of possibility. I shall be in no way surprised if in case there be existent upon Mars beings of an intelligence analogous to that of human beings, they find a means of getting into communication with us on this planet."

Marconi added, "Immense things remain to be learned. It would be foolish to suppose ... that life cannot exist under conditions other than terrestrial, that is under conditions different from those existing on this planet. It is certainly within the bounds of possibility."

In conclusion, it is fascinating that two of the world's greatest scientists of their era, Tesla and Marconi, both believed they were receiving signals from some unknown source in outer space, possibly on Mars or Venus. Could their initial assessment have been valid?

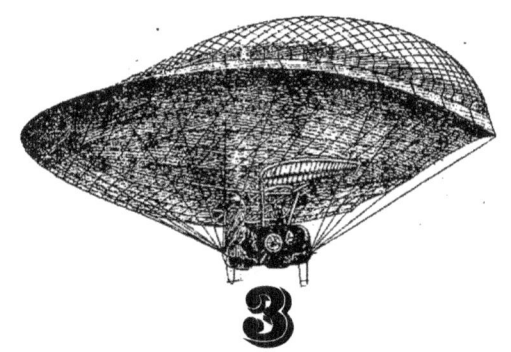

3
CELESTIAL STARFISH
April 10, 1901
Anaconda, Montana

A UFO SHAPED like a horseshoe may seem odd, but what about a flying object shaped like a starfish? Although the local newspaper called it a "flying ghost," a starfish-shaped UFO seems to be what people saw in Anaconda, Montana, on April 10, 1901.

The town was founded in 1883, named after the Anaconda copper mine that had been established in the area. On the evening of Wednesday, April 10, witnesses heard a "whirring, whizzing, swishing" sound in the skies above the town.

EARLY 20th CENTURY UFOs

Upon looking up, they saw, at an altitude of about 1,000 feet, a "mighty dark object sailing or soaring high in the air, its course being northerly."

> A flying ghost is the latest wonder to agitate the good people of the hill city. Last night while the sky was clear a whirring, whizzing, swishing sound in the heavens attracted the attention of the meek and lowly who "rubbered" and beheld a mighty dark object sailing or soaring high in the air, its course being northerly. It was estimated that the thing was about 36 feet from tip to tip, but its shape was not that of a bird, or bat, or butterfly. It resembled in general outline a huge star fish. It was calculated to be about 1,000 feet high, and it moved slowly. The strange sound grew less in intensity until only a mild whisper likened unto a zephyr toying with the tender leaves of a quaking asp told of the passing of the mystery. Men stood out of doors until long after midnight watching the heavens, hoping in vain to catch another glimpse of the strange object.

The Anaconda (Montana) Standard, April 11th, 1901, page 10

The strange object, shaped like "a huge star fish," was about 36 feet in diameter ("from tip to tip") and was moving very slowly, according to a newspaper account in the *Anaconda (Montana) Standard.*

The shape of the object was of particular interest to the observers, and the newspaper account stated that "its shape was not that of a bird, or bat, or butterfly. It resembled in general outline a huge star fish."

AMERICAN SIGHTINGS: 1900-1919

Part of the Anaconda Copper Mining Company in 1919 (NARA)

The sound from the object continued, although it diminished in intensity as the craft passed by. "The strange sound grew less in intensity until only a mild whisper likened unto a zephyr toying with the tender leaves of a quaking asp told of the passing of the mystery."

In terms of witnesses, the newspaper account mentioned that the UFO was seen by many of the local men and for quite a long period of time. "Men stood out of doors until long after midnight watching the heavens, hoping in vain to catch another glimpse of the strange object."

Since this was another nighttime sighting and the UFO was described as "mighty dark," it is possible that the witness description of the object was not precise. The craft obviously had a hub and spoke configuration with several "arms" extending out from a central core. It may have even, perhaps, been a so-called "black triangle" UFO, which might have looked like a starfish to the people of 1901.

EARLY 20th CENTURY UFOs

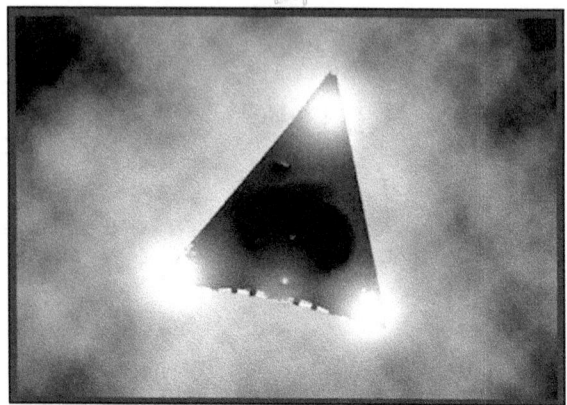

Artist's Rendition of a Black Triangle UFO

Or, then again, perhaps it *was* really shaped like a starfish!

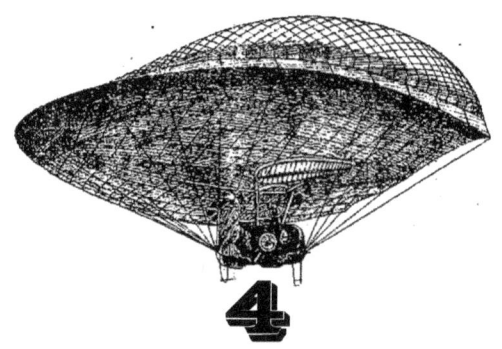

4
THE VAN METER VISITORS
September & October 1903
Van Meter, Iowa

IN SEPTEMBER and October 1903, about 20 miles west of Des Moines, Iowa, in the tiny town of Van Meter, there arose one of the most bizarre "creature" stories ever. It involved a strange, winged beast, possibly extraterrestrial, that was seen by multiple witnesses at several different locations. Van Meter had a population of 407 in the 1900 census and seems an unlikely place for a paranormal incident of this magnitude to have occurred. Yet the event is still remembered and celebrated today.

The incident began when Van Meter resident Uly Griffith, a traveling tool salesman, returned to his hometown after midnight on September 29,

EARLY 20ᵗʰ CENTURY UFOs

1903. He noticed a strange light atop one of the neighboring buildings, which he thought was suspicious. Walking closer to the light, he saw that it moved with amazing speed to another roof across the street. Puzzled, Griffith then noticed that the mysterious light suddenly disappeared altogether.

The next incident happened about 24 hours later, early in the morning of September 30. The town physician, Dr. A. C. Olcott, was awakened by a bright light shining in his face. Grabbing his gun and going outside to look for the source of the light, Olcott saw what looked like a half-human, half-animal creature with "great bat-like wings" and a "single blunt horn" on the forehead. It became clear to Olcott that the bright light was coming from the creature's horn.

Train Station in Van Meter, Iowa, in 1907
Olson Photograph Co. (Plattsmouth, Neb.) / CC
BY-SA (https://creativecommons.org/licenses/by-sa/4.0)

AMERICAN SIGHTINGS: 1900-1919

Shocked and frightened, Olcott raised his weapon and fired five times, striking the creature. Shockingly, the bullets had absolutely no effect on the beast. Alcott quickly retreated into his office, locking the door securely behind him.

*Sketch of Creature
(Courtesy Van Meter Public Library)*

EARLY 20th CENTURY UFOs

The creature made another appearance during the early morning hours of October 1, when it was seen by Clarence "Peter" Dunn, who worked at the town's bank and watched the bank building at night. Armed with a shotgun, he was soon alerted to strange gurgling noises outside the bank. Through the front window, he saw a very bright light shining upon him, which he later saw was coming from the bizarre creature. He fired the shotgun, shattering the glass of the front window, but the creature disappeared. He later discovered large, three-toed tracks where the creature had stepped in the soft earth.

DES MOINES' NEW MONSTER

Citizens Tell Weird Tales of This Modern Terror.

Des Moines, Oct. 12.—According to prominent citizens, two weird-looking, terror-striking monsters are living in an abandoned coal mine on the edge of the town. At night they come out and act as a sort of town curfew bell—every one locks the doors and hides under beds or behind curtains. Residents whose veracity heretofore has been unquestioned tell harrowing stories of experiences with the horrible monsters.

Dr. A. C. Olcott, awakened by a bright light shining through his window, says the terror he saw was half human and half beast, with great bat-like wings. A dazzling light that fairly blinded him came from a blunt, horn-like protuberance in the middle of the animal's forehead, and it gave off a stupefying odor that almost overcame him.

Peter Dunn, cashier of the bank, fired his shotgun at the monster. Next morning imprints of great three-toed feet were discernible in the soft earth. Plaster casts of them were taken.

Dr. O. V. White saw the monster climbing down a telephone pole, using a beak much in the manner of a parrot. As it struck the ground it seemed to travel in leaps, featherless wings to assist. It gave off no light. He fired at it, and he believes he wounded it. The shot was followed by an overpowering odor.

Sidney Gregg, attracted by the shot, saw the monster flying away.

J. L. Pratt, foreman of the brick plant, heard a peculiar sound in an abandoned coal mine. Presently the monster emerged from the shaft, accompanied by a smaller one. A score of shots were fired without effect.

The whole town was aroused and just at dawn the two monsters returned and disappeared down the shaft.

The Courier of Waterloo, Iowa
Oct. 12, 1903, p. 1

Late that same evening, the creature was spotted once more, this time by O.V. White, who kept lodgings in an upstairs room of the hardware and furniture store that he co-owned. Grabbing his gun, White soon located the mysterious creature crouching on the crossbar of a nearby telephone pole. White fired at the creature and thought he had wounded it, but with little apparent effect. Interestingly, White said the creature emitted an odor or vapor that seemed to "stupefy" him. A variation of one of the articles also seemed to imply that White had trouble remembering events, as it said that after being disorientated by the odor that "he remembered no more about it." This statement is open to interpretation, of course, but ufologists could associate this statement with the missing time phenomena common to many abductees.

The sound of White's gunshot brought another local storeowner, Sidney Gregg, out to see what was happening. Gregg saw the creature, which he described as being at least 8-feet tall with the light on its horn being as bright as an "electric headlight." Gregg said the creature flapped its wings and leaped like a kangaroo, at one point standing erect on two feet before dropping down to all fours and springing away. It then took flight with its wings, seemingly headed to an abandoned coal mine at the edge of town.

Early on the morning of October 3, a worker at a nearby tile and brick factory, J. L. Platt, Jr., heard strange noises coming from the vicinity of the coal mine and went to investigate. The sounds led him to where the bizarre creature was lurking, accompanied by a second, somewhat smaller beast of the same type!

Seeing Platt, the creatures ran away, Platt headed into town to let everyone know that he had

EARLY 20th CENTURY UFOs

discovered the lair of some type of horrible monsters. A posse was assembled, and it headed down to the mine to await the appearance of the creatures.

At around dawn, the armed posse saw the two winged monstrosities approaching the mine, and the men opened fire. Unfazed by the hail of bullets, the creatures easily moved past the men and made their way deep into the old mine, where the men were unwilling to follow.

The story ends with the townspeople deciding to barricade the mine entrance and trap the unearthly beasts inside. No further information has been found about what happened in the end, including whether the barricade idea worked. Apparently, the creatures were never seen again.

Abandoned Mine
Famartin / CC BY-SA
(https://creativecommons.org/licenses/by-sa/3.0)

AMERICAN SIGHTINGS: 1900-1919

Some UFO researchers over the years have wondered if the "monsters" may have actually been humanoids wearing some type of special suit, such as an astronaut might wear. Is it possible that the extremely bright light coming from the "horn" in the middle of the forehead was really a head lamp attached seamlessly to some type of helmet?

What if these creatures had landed in a spaceship nearby and were exploring the area wearing specialized gear to help them cope with the unknown atmosphere? It also seems at least conceivable that they were a type of robot or android, since they were impervious to bullets.

In more recent years, the town of Van Meter has taken a page from places like Roswell, New Mexico, famous for its UFO crash, and Point Pleasant, West Virginia, the home of Mothman, to create the Van Meter Visitor Festival, which debuted in 2018.

EARLY 20th CENTURY UFOs

SMELTER IS HAUNTED

GHOST OR DEVIL APPEARED AT LANYON SMELTER SATURDAYNIGHT TWICE.

SCARED NIGHT MEN TO DEATH

The Thing Appeared at Furnace No. 9 Works No. 1—Had oHrns and Its Head Floated in Air—Man Who Saw It Collapsed in a Heap and Daylight Was Awaited Before Night Force Went Home.

A ghost appeared last Saturday night in furnace No. 9 at Works No. 1 of the Lanyon Zinc Company, and to this day nobody knows the truth about it.

The night shift was working at the furnace when the Thing appeared just about midnight. When first seen it was standing beside the furnace, between No. 9 and the adjoining one. The man who saw it gave a yell and fled. The other men ran to the place to see what was wrong and all took one look at the Thing and away they went. The front man fell down and the others fell over him. Afterward they screwed up their courage and returned and it was gone.

Little else was talked of for some time. The Thing had horns and long hair, great big eyes and an inhuman look, although standing erect like a man. It was a Spirit or the Devil. Before the excitement had subsided one of the men went to a window at the west side of the furnace room and opened the window. Merciful heavens! There it was! The man sank in a heap. Another workman walked over and threw a chistle at the Thing's head. It did not dodge, nor run, but came forward. When it disappeared again it stayed away. The night metal drawers and stuffers, although through their work at 3 o'clock, remained until daylight before going home.

Among the men working that night were Chris Klamick, who was overcome; Ed. Mundis, John Rice and Len Hartley were also on the shift. The boys have kept very quiet about the Thing, but they won't deny that it scared the livers out of them, and they have a constant fear that it may come back.

Whether the apparition is the Evil Spirit of the Gas, or some man masquerading for the fun of it, the men neither know nor care. But they know the Thing—the inhuman, awful Think—stood there. Ghost, Devil or man, they do not care to renew acquaintance.

Iola (Kansas) Daily Register and Evening News, Nov. 18, 1903, p. 1

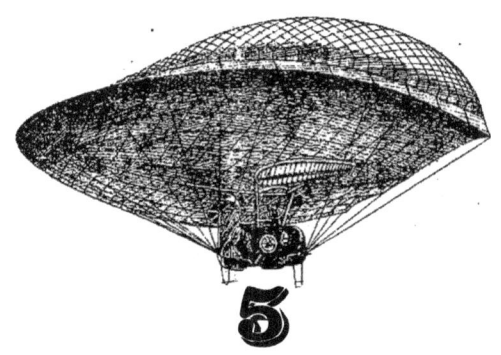

5
THE THING IN THE MINE
November 14, 1903
Iola, Kansas

THE ENTITY WE are about to discuss brings to mind some of the very tall aliens that appeared in 1896 in Lodi, California, and in 1897 in Reynolds, Michigan (covered in our book *The Coming of the Airships*). Perhaps one of these aliens was still hanging about the planet in 1903? Or, considering the vastly different description of the "thing in the mine," this creature was probably something entirely unique. Zinc miners in Iola, Kansas, reported seeing an incredibly horrific looking creature down in Furnace Number 9 of the Lanyon Zinc Smelter on November 14, 1903.

The newspaper account in the November 18 edition of the *Iola (Kansas) Daily Register and*

EARLY 20th CENTURY UFOs

Evening News stated that the nightshift miners were hard at work at the smelting facilities of the Lanyon Zinc Company when something unbelievable happened. It was near midnight on a Saturday, when several of the workers noticed a tall humanoid standing between two of the furnaces used to smelt zinc ore.

Zinc Smelter Workers in Iola, Kansas - Date Unknown (Courtesy EPA.gov)

Referred to simply as "The Thing," the strange creature stood erect like a man, sported long hair, looked at the miners through huge eyes, and had horns atop its head! The men who first saw the creature let out a chorus of yells, which brought the other smelter workers running to see what the commotion was about.

Once all the men got a careful look at what they were dealing with, a mad scramble to exit the smelter ensued. One unfortunate miner stumbled, falling upon the ground, and was mercilessly trampled by his colleagues as they speedily vacated the premises.

For quite some time after the encounter, the workers talked about nothing else, discussing at length what they had witnessed. The newspaper account said, "Little else was talked of for some time. The Thing had horns and long hair, great big eyes and an inhuman body although standing erect like a man. It was a spirit or the Devil."

Motivated to solve the mystery, the miners "screwed up their courage" and returned to the area of their earlier sighting. But the terrifying creature was gone.

Photo of the Lanyon Zinc Works, Date Unknown

As the evening wore on, one of the workers, Chris Klemick, was opening one of windows of the furnace room, when he saw the creature once again. Klemick immediately fainted. One of the

EARLY 20th CENTURY UFOs

other workers, picked up a heavy chisel and heaved it at the Thing's head. "Before the excitement had subsided, one of the men went to a window on the west side of the furnace room and opened the window. Merciful heavens! There it was! The man sank in a heap. Another workman walked over and threw a chisel at the Thing's head. It did not dodge, nor run, but came forwards. When it disappeared again, it stayed away," according to the newspaper account.

Zinc Smelting Operation in Iola, Kansas - Date Unknown (EPA.gov)

The newspaper noted that even though some of the smelter workers ended their shift at 3 a.m., they did not leave the zinc works for fear of running into the creature on their way out. Instead, the workers stayed indoors until daybreak before finding the courage to return to their homes.

AMERICAN SIGHTINGS: 1900-1919

The miners involved in the encounter were actually identified by name in the newspaper article: "Among the men working that night were Chris Klemick, who was overcome; Ed. Mundis, John Rice and Len Hartley were also on the shift."

For a time, the workers kept quiet about their experience. "The boys have kept very quiet about the Thing, but they won't deny that it scared the livers out of them, and they have a constant fear that it may come back."

Added the paper, "Whether the apparition is the Evil Spirit of the Gas, or some man masquerading for the fun of it, the men neither know nor care. But they know the Thing -- the inhuman, awful Thing -- stood there. Ghost or Devil or man, they do not care to renew acquaintance." The newspaper article concluded, "To this day, nobody knows the truth about it."

What was this strange creature? Was it a denizen of outer space or the inner Earth? We know of several interesting UFO cases in Kansas during the 19th century – so perhaps the creature was left behind or missed its ride back home? A search of the historical record for more sightings of this strange humanoid resulted in no further data.

EARLY 20th CENTURY UFOs

The U.S.S. Supply in August 1902
(U.S. Navy Photo)

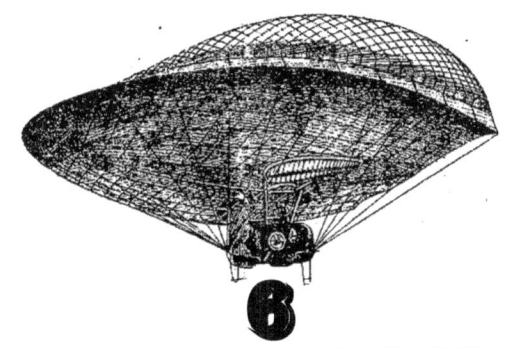

NAVY SHIP ENCOUNTERS UFOs

February 24, 1904
Atlantic Ocean Near San Francisco

IN 1904, the United States Navy vessel, the *U.S.S. Supply*, was en route from Guam to San Francisco, California, when it encountered a formation of three UFOs, flying very high and very fast, over the ship in the Atlantic Ocean. The sighting was documented by the ship's commander, Lieutenant Frank H. Schofield, U.S.N., in a report carried by numerous U.S. newspapers and in the March 1904 issue of the U.S. Weather Bureau's monthly publication, *Weather Review*. The sighting was later given as an example of pre-1947 UFO cases in Donald Keyhoe's landmark 1950 book, *The Flying Saucers Are Real*, on page 61.

EARLY 20ᵗʰ CENTURY UFOs

SUPPLY SAILS TOMORROW.

The U. S. S. Supply will sail for San Francisco tomorrow morning. When the vessel arrived here the health of Governor Sewall of Guam, who is on board, was in such poor state that it was deemed too risky for him to continue the voyage to San Francisco.

During the stay in port Governor Sewall has improved considerably and it is now thought that he can stand the voyage to San Francisco, where he will seek the best of expert medical aid.

Honolulu (Hawaii) Evening Bulletin, Feb. 19, 1904, p. 4

Our story of the Navy vessel's UFO encounter begins with its departure on February 20, 1904 from Honolulu, Hawaii, after a stopover in its journey from Guam to San Francisco. On board the ship was an ailing dignitary, William Elbridge Sewell, United States Navy Lieutenant Commander and the 6th Naval Governor of Guam. Sewell had fallen gravely ill and was trying to make it back to the U.S. for medical treatment. Unfortunately, he died shortly after making this voyage, passing away on March 18, 1904, at Mare Island, California.

AMERICAN SIGHTINGS: 1900-1919

An article that appeared in the *Minneapolis (Minnesota) Star Tribune* on March 9, 1904, disclosed the sighting of the strange UFOs, and although the article refers to them as "meteors," it is clear from their appearance and trajectory that they were very likely not meteors. Readers should keep in mind that in 1904, the term "unidentified flying object" was unknown, and the military had no system for reporting objects that did not fit into the normal scheme of things. Airplanes had not been invented yet and what the U.S.S. Supply crew saw was obviously not a balloon or dirigible. So, anything seen streaking across the sky was immediately labeled a "meteor," regardless of its true nature. "Wondrous meteors" is what one reporter called what the U.S.S. Supply witnessed.

The sighting occurred when the ship was approximately 300 nautical miles from San Francisco Bay. It had already travelled about 1,700 nautical miles from Honolulu and was closing in on the California coast. Suddenly, three members of the ship's crew witnessed a formation of three UFOs moving rapidly toward the ship's position from the north-northwest.

The three objects were bright red in color, the largest being egg-shaped and about six times the size of the sun in the sky. The second and third objects were round, rather than egg shaped, and the objects "showed no imperfections in shape." The second object was about twice the size of the sun. The third object was about the same size as the sun, observed from Earth.

EARLY 20th CENTURY UFOs

The formation of UFOs, rising from below the clouds to well above the clouds, zoomed over the ship, being at one point perhaps a mile above it and viewable at a 45-degree angle from the deck of the ship. After zooming past the ship, they continued toward the west-northwest and shifted to a 75-degree angle in the sky, relative to the ship, indicating that they had risen in altitude, eliminating the possibility that they were meteors.

The sighting lasted a total of two minutes, and no satisfactory explanation as to what the objects could have been was ever given.

> **METEORS PLAINLY SEEN**
>
> LIEUT. SCHOFIELD, U. S. N., DESCRIBES UNIQUE VIEW.
>
> Bright Red in Color, Three Meteors Soar Above the Clouds at an Elevation of About Forty-five Degrees—Observed Feb. 28 by Three Persons on Board U. S. S. Supply, From Guam to San Francisco.
>
> WASHINGTON, March 9.—In a report to the navy department received yesterday Lieut. Frank H. Schofield, U. S. N., commanding the U. S. S. Supply from Guam for San Francisco, tells of the observance of February 28 in latitude 35 degrees 58 minutes north, longitude 128 degrees 36 minutes west, of three meteors which he says appeared in a group from northwest by the north directly toward the supply.
>
> Lieut. Schofield reports that at first their angular motion was rapid and color a rather bright red. As they approached the ship they appeared to soar above the clouds at an elevation of about 45 degrees. He says that after raising above the clouds their angular motion became less and less until it ceased when they appeared to be moving directly away from the earth at an elevation of about 75 degrees, and in a direction west northwest.
>
> The largest meteor had an apparent area of about six suns. It was egg shaped, the sharper end forward. The second and third meteors were round and showed no imperfections in shape. The second meteor was estimated to be twice the size of the sun in appearance and the third meteor about a mile above the ship. They were observed by three persons, and were in sight for two minutes.
>
> *Star Tribune (Minneapolis, Minnesota)*
> *Mar. 9, 1904, p. 1*

The *Star Tribune* article said, "In a report to the navy department received yesterday Lieut. Frank H. Schofield, U.S.N., commanding the U.S.S. Supply from Guam for San Francisco, tells of the observance of February 28 in latitude 35 degrees 58 minutes north, longitude 128 degrees 36 minutes west, of three meteors which he says appeared in a group from northwest by the north directly toward the Supply."

> The monthly weather bureau publishes a summary of the observations covering three remarkable meteors observed by the U. S. S. Supply at sea on February 28 last. The meteors appeared in a group, the largest having an "apparent area of about six suns." It was egg-shaped, the sharper end forward. This end was jagged in outline. The other two meteors were round, one apparently "double the size of the sun" and the other "about the size of the sun."

The Scranton (Pennsylvania) Republican, July 9, 1904, p. 3

The *Star Tribune* article continued, "Lieut. Schofield reports that at first their angular motion was rapid and color a rather bright red. As they approached the ship, they appeared to soar above the clouds at an elevation of about 45 degrees. He says that after raising above the clouds their angular motion became less and less until it ceased when they appeared to be moving directly away from the earth at an elevation of about 75 degrees, and in a direction west northwest."

The report concluded, "The largest meteor had an apparent area of about six suns. It was egg shaped, the sharper end forward. The second and third meteors were round and showed no imperfections in shape. The second meteor was estimated to be twice the size of the sun in

EARLY 20th CENTURY UFOs

appearance and the third meteor about a mile above the ship. They were observed by three persons and were in sight for two minutes."

Certainly one of the most dramatic early 20th century UFO sightings, this 1904 encounter featured multiple craft, multiple witnesses, and observers that are considered highly reliable. The remarkable nature of this event continues to impress UFO researchers even today, and it was surely a dramatic way to inaugurate the 20th century.

BIGGER THAN THE SUN

Lieut. Schofield Sees Three Wondrous Meteors.

WASHINGTON, D. C., March 8.—In a report to the navy department received today Lieut. Frank H. Schofield, U. S. N., commanding the U. S. S. Supply, from Guam for San Francisco, tells of the observance, on Feb. 8, in latitude 35 degrees 58 minutes north, longitude 128 degrees 36 minutes west, of three meteors, which, he says, appeared near the horizon and below the clouds, traveling in a group from northwest by north directly toward the Supply.

At first their angular motion was rapid and of a rather bright red. As they approached the ship they appeared to soar above the clouds at an elevation of 45 degrees. After rising above the clouds their angular motion became less and less until it ceased, when they appeared to be moving directly away from the earth at an elevation of about 75 degrees and in a direction west-northwest.

The largest meteor had an apparent area of six suns. It was egg-shaped the sharper end forward. The second and third meteors were round and showed no imperfections in shape. The second meteor was estimated to be twice the size of the sun in appearance, and the third meteor about the size of the sun. It is estimated the meteors were a mile above the ship. They were observed by three persons and were in sight two minutes.

The Saint Paul (Minnesota) Globe, 3-9-1904, p. 3

THE FIRST PHILADELPHIA EXPERIMENT

August 1, 1904
Philadelphia, Pennsylvania

MANY PARANORMAL researchers point to a very strange incident that occurred in October 1943 called "The Philadelphia Experiment." Reportedly, the U.S. Navy conducted a military experiment to make an entire naval vessel, the *USS Eldridge*, completely invisible, or "cloaked." Some researchers claim that the experiment caused the ship and its crew to become surrounded by a strange electromagnetic anomaly that allegedly transported the ship and its crew backward or forward in time.

EARLY 20th CENTURY UFOs

SHIP CLAD IN VAPOR FRIGHTENS THE CREW

Strange Experience of Sailors on Steamer Mohican Near Delaware Breakwater—Compass Disabled.

PHILADELPHIA, Pa., Aug. 2.—When the British steamer Mohican, Captain Urquhart, from Ibraila, Roumania, in this port, was making for the Delaware Breakwater it had a most remarkable experience, which terrorized the crew, played havoc with the ship's compass and brought the vessel to a standstill for nearly half an hour.

For that length of time the Mohican was enshrouded in a strange metallic vapor, which glowed like phosphorus. The entire vessel looked as if it were on fire and the sailors flitted about the deck like glowing phantoms.

The cloud has a strange magnetic effect on the vessel, for the needle of the compass revolved with the speed of an electric motor, and the sailors were unable to raise pieces of steel from the magnetized decks.

Strange Gray Cloud.

"It was shortly after the sun had gone," Captain Urquhart said. "The sea was almost as level as a parlor carpet, and scarcely a breeze ruffled the water. It was slowly growing dark when the lookout saw a strange gray cloud in the southeast. At first it appeared as a speck on the horizon, but it rapidly came nearer, and was soon as large as a balloon.

"It had a peculiar gray tinge, and as it bore down upon us we saw bright glowing spots on its mass. Suddenly the cloud enveloped the ship, and the Mohican blazed forth like a ship on fire, and from stem to stern and topmast to keel everything was tinged with the strange glow.

"The seamen were in terror. Their hair stood straight on end, not from the fright so much as from the magnetic power of the cloud. They rushed about the deck in consternation and the more they rushed about the more excited they became. I tried to calm them, but the situation was beyond me.

The Needle Flying.

"I looked at the needle and it was flying around like an electric fan. I ordered several of the crew to move some iron chains that were lying on the deck, thinking it would distract their attention. But the sailors could not budge the chains, although they did not weigh more than seventy-five pounds each. Everything was magnetized, and chains, bolts, spikes, and bars were as tight on the deck as if they had been riveted there.

"For half an hour we were enveloped in that mysterious vapor, and for nearly all that time, after the sailors' first cries of fright had subsided, there was a great silence over everything that only added to the terror. I tried to talk, but the words refused to leave my lips. The density of the cloud was so great that it would not carry sound.

"Suddenly the cloud began to lift. The phosphorescent glow of the ship and the crew began to fade. It gradually died away and in a few minutes the cloud had passed over the vessel and we saw it moving off over the sea."

The Washington (D.C.) Times, Aug. 2, 1904, p. 7

As odd as it may sound, an eerily similar phenomenon was observed near Philadelphia four decades earlier, in 1904, as an entire ship suddenly became fully surrounded by a strange electromagnetic force that was unleashed upon it by a bizarre cloud-like object floating above it. Could it have somehow been related to the 1943 Philadelphia Experiment? It seems a striking

AMERICAN SIGHTINGS: 1900-1919

coincidence that both events occurred in the same general area.

On August 1, 1904, the British steamer *Mohican*, registered in what is now called Bralia, Romania, had just left port in Philadelphia, headed south toward the Delaware Breakwater. The extremely unusual circumstances that followed were reported by the ship's captain, identified only as "Captain Urquhard," in an article that appeared in the *Washington (D.C.) Times* on August 2.

Shortly after leaving Philadelphia, the article said, the *Mohican* was steaming on a calm sea with hardly a breeze, as the sun set and night fell. The captain said, "The sea was almost as level as a parlor carpet, and scarcely a breeze ruffled the water. It was slowly growing dark when the lookout saw a strange gray cloud in the southeast. At first, it appeared as a speck on the horizon, but it rapidly came nearer and was soon as large as a balloon [probably referring to a hot air balloon or other type of dirigible]." As previously noted in this book series, UFOs are often said to "cloak" themselves within clouds or to assume a cloud-like appearance. It is uncertain whether the cloud that approached the Mohican was some type of aerial craft, but it definitely was a kind of aerial anomaly.

Captain Urquhart's description of the strange cloud is particularly striking: "It had a peculiar gray tinge, and as it bore down upon us, we saw bright glowing spots on its mass." The glowing spots of light that shone through the cloud mass could possibly indicate a lighted aerial craft hidden in the cloud.

EARLY 20th CENTURY UFOs

What happened next filled the *Mohican's* crew with absolute terror for nearly half an hour, as some type of energy was imparted from the cloud down to the ship below, and the naval vessel was "enshrouded" in a strange ball of energy that caused a series of electromagnetic anomalies to occur on board the ship.

A Similar British Steamer, 1904 (Wikimedia)

During the 30 minute span, the ship came to a standstill, the navigational compass spun wildly, and all metal objects on the ship became magnetized and strongly attached to the ship's deck. The entire ship "looked as if it were on fire and the sailors flitted about the deck like glowing phantoms."

According to Captain Urquhard, "the needle of the compass revolved with the speed of an electric motor, and the sailors were unable to raise pieces of steel from the magnetized decks." About the spinning compass, he said, "I looked at the needle and it was flying around like an electric fan."

Electrical Disturbance (JPlenio / Pixabay)

Paranormal investigators have suggested that the ship was being "sucked" into an inter-dimensional portal or perhaps a portal in time.

Captain Urquhard later told reporters, "The seamen were in terror. Their hair stood straight on end, not from the fright so much as from the magnetic power of the cloud. They rushed about the deck in consternation and the more they rushed about, the more excited they became. I tried to calm them, but the situation was beyond me." The captain added that many of his crew began praying for their safety and the ship's safety.

The captain said, "I ordered several of the crew to move some iron chains that were lying on the deck, thinking it would distract their attention. But the sailors could not budge the chains, although they did not weigh more than seventy-five pounds each. Everything was magnetized, and chains, bolts, spikes, and bars were as tight on the deck as if they had been riveted there."

As the strange energy settled in more forcefully, the crew were unable to speak to each other. "For half an hour we were enveloped in that mysterious vapor, and for nearly all that time, after the sailors' first cries of fright had subsided, there was a great silence over everything that only added to the terror. I tried to talk, but the words refused to leave my lips. The density of the cloud was so great that it would not carry sound."

The historical record does not indicate that the crew suffered any time displacement or other after effects of their experience. Captain Urquhard stated that the event concluded as follows: "Suddenly the cloud began to lift. The phosphorescent glow of the ship and the crew began to fade. It gradually died away and in a few minutes, the cloud had passed over the vessel, and we were moving off over the sea."

Could this have been some type of residual effect from the Philadelphia Experiment that was conducted some 39 years later? Was the Mohican somehow trapped in some kind of displacement wave from the 1943 experiment? Did the *USS Eldridge* momentarily appear near the *Mohican*, causing the displacement? So many questions, but again, so few answers.

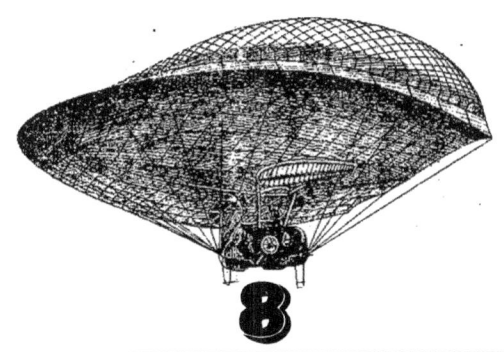

THE "THING" FROZEN IN ICE
October 27, 1904
Sitka, Alaska

THE AUGUST 1938 edition of the highly acclaimed early science fiction magazine *Astounding Science Fiction* contained a short novel titled "Who Goes There?" about an extraterrestrial creature found buried in the Antarctic ice, having been frozen there following the crash of its spaceship centuries before. Written by the magazine's editor, John W. Campbell, Jr., under the pseudonym Don A. Stuart, the story told of what happened when the creature thawed out and tried to take over an Antarctic research base. The story greatly influenced the science fiction genre and spawned three major motion pictures.

EARLY 20th CENTURY UFOs

Sketch of Humanoid Found Frozen in Ice

AMERICAN SIGHTINGS: 1900-1919

It also may have been based on an event that supposedly happened in Lake Tinsel, Alaska, on October 27, 1904. Newspaper reports claimed that a "queer being" was found frozen in an iceberg and that the strange, mummy-like creature was brought back to life!

Opening Pages of the 1938 John W. Campbell story (Archive.org)

In an article from the *Philadelphia Inquirer* on November 5, 1904, the discovery of the strange creature was first announced in a dispatch from Alaska dated October 27: "NOT ANIMAL -- NOT HUMAN -- WHAT IS IT? Astounding Discovery of a Queer Being Preserved for Thousands of Years in an Iceberg."

The dispatch said, "Much excitement was caused last night when an Esquimaux [Eskimo] runner brought in the news of a strange being – not animal, and yet apparently not human -- discovered in an

EARLY 20th CENTURY UFOs

iceberg a short distance from the dog-trail that skirts Lake Tinsel. The iceberg was first seen floating some distance from shore by servants of the household of Elgnirk Ssirk, the noted scientist and traveler, while returning from a spearing expedition in the Conjure region. For unexplained reasons they were using the old dog-route, bordering Lake Tinsel, long ago abandoned because of danger."

The tale continued, "An attempt was made to get near the berg, but without success. Returning to the home of Mr. Ssirk, his servants told him what they had seen. Procuring rope and gunpowder, Mr. Ssirk started at once for the lake, accompanied by his servants. It was a ten-mile journey back, and when the party arrived the berg had approached much nearer the shore. Through the crystal ice

---

NOT ANIMAL—NOT HUMAN—WHAT IS IT?

Astounding Discovery of a Queer Being Preserved for Thousands of Years in an Iceberg

THINK LIFE MAY EXIST

(Special Correspondence)

SITKA, Alaska, Oct. 28.

Much excitement was caused last night when an Esquimaux runner brought in the news of a strange being—not animal, and yet apparently not human—discovered in an iceberg a short distance from the dog-trail that skirts Lake Tinsel.

The iceberg was first seen floating some distance from shore by servants of the household of Elgnirk Ssirk, the noted scientist and traveler, while returning from a spearing expedition in the Conjure region. For unexplained reasons they were using the old dog-route, bordering Lake Tinsel, long ago abandoned because of danger.

Not Animal, Not Human

An attempt was made to get near the berg, but without success. Returning to the home of Mr. Ssirk, his servants told him what they had seen. Procuring rope and gunpowder, Mr. Ssirk started at once for the lake, accompanied by his servants.

It was a ten-mile journey back, and when the party arrived the berg had approached much nearer the shore. Through the crystal ice could be seen the form inside. It was unlike that of any known animal, yet was apparently not human.

Farther than this nothing has been heard about the strange incident, and it was only because of the fear of one of the servants of Mr. Ssirk, who fled back to his quarters and hid himself there, after telling what he had seen, that this much information can now be forwarded.

May be Resuscitated

Much speculation has arisen here as to whether a living body could be preserved in ice for thousands of years without change of form, and an attempt will be made to resuscitate the "thing" if it can be taken out of the ice without injury.

I will forward another letter as soon as further news is received.

The Philadelphia (Pennsylvania) Inquirer, Nov. 5, 1904, p. 8

AMERICAN SIGHTINGS: 1900-1919

could be seen the form inside. It was unlike that of any known animal yet was apparently not human."

As in the fictional story by John W. Campbell, Jr., a strange creature was spotted frozen in ice and then efforts were made to extract it. The discovery of the creature was apparently so upsetting to the men who found it that one of them fled in horror back to his quarters and hid himself there.

The newspaper article concluded, "Much speculation has arisen here as to whether a living body could be preserved in ice for thousands of years without change of form, and an attempt will be made to resuscitate the 'thing' if it can be taken out of the ice without injury. I will forward another letter as soon as further news is received."

Three days later, the *Philadelphia Inquirer* carried an update to the story proclaiming "ALIVE AND TALKING, THE ICEBERG 'THING – Like a Mummy in Day, but Lively at Night – Mr. Ssirk Faints Under Strain. First Meal for Years."

This second dispatch, dated November 1, said, "Enclosed with this letter is a sketch by Mr. Elgnirk Ssirk of the queer 'thing' found encased in an iceberg on Lake Tinsel. Last night a party of Esquimaux [Inuit] runners highly excited dashed into Sitka and reported that the mysterious creature had come to life, that Mr. Ssirk was ill from the strain and that many of his servants had fled. Business in Sitka is temporarily suspended. Many persons are already on the dog-trail to the interior and a party of one hundred and fifty men left here this morning on skis for the Ssirk estate."

EARLY 20th CENTURY UFOs

ALIVE AND TALKING, THE ICEBERG "THING"

Like a Mummy in Day, but Lively at Night—Mr. Ssirk Faints Under Strain.

FIRST MEAL FOR YEARS

(Special Correspondence)
SITKA, Alaska, Nov 1st, 1904.

The reporter continued, "My Esquimaux informants state that for nearly an hour after its release the creature lay like a mummy. Then, as night fell, the eyelids quivered, and rheum was seen to issue from them. All the while Mr. Ssirk was engaged in massaging the thing's wrists and heart. With the coming dusk animation stirred its body. The lips trembled; the fingers shook nervously. Suddenly as the moon rose, the tongue protruded, and articulation was heard."

The resurrection of the creature supposedly caused Ssirk to faint, but after he felt better, he saw an amazing sight. "Recovering, Mr. Ssirk saw again the weird being and found it wholly alive and seated on a chair like any human creature, dispatching

AMERICAN SIGHTINGS: 1900-1919

with gluttonous haste all the visible eatables on the servant's table; its first food for possibly 4,000 years."

The reporter added, "My Esquimaux messengers added that when daylight came the creature acted as one dead, and remained so until nightfall, when it emerged from its coma, and, bearing itself like a high-caste human, uttered strange speech and made overt attempts to convey its thoughts."

The article closed with the reporter promising to provide another update soon, but a week later, the newspaper complained, "For some unknown reason, our correspondent at Sitka, Alaska, from whom we expected further word concerning the developments of the iceberg mystery, has failed to forward news of any sort. We are at a total loss to understand the total absence of further advices."

On November 11, an article appeared in the same newspaper from Mrs. Elgnirk Ssirk, the wife of the explorer who was involved in finding the frozen creature. She disclosed that she had been the correspondent that had been sending dispatches about the discovery to the Philadelphia Inquirer. She also announced that she and her husband were heading back to Philadelphia and were bringing along "our curious charges, found in the icebergs."

Finally, on November 12, the entire deception was revealed. The newspaper announced a line of toy dolls called "Gollywogs" supposedly found in icebergs by *Kriss Kringle* (Elgnirk Ssirk spelled backwards) – in other words, Santa Claus. The entire episode was a foolish marketing scheme by a department store called Wanamaker.

Although no truthfulness was found in this wacky hoax from 1904, it seems possible that the bizarre episode may have been seen by John W. Campbell, Jr., leading him to write one of the most enduring science-fiction stories of our time, *Who Goes There?*

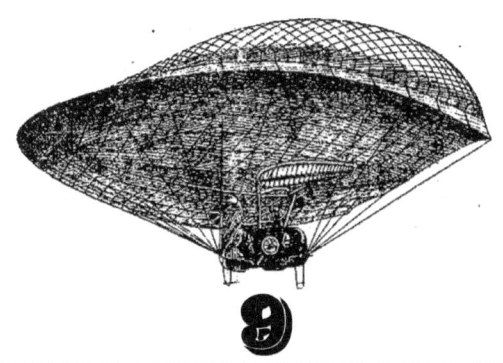

MYSTERY METEOR IN NEW YORK
March 14 - 15, 1906
Rochester, New York

BEGINNING ON THE EVENING of March 14, 1906 and continuing through the next morning, a "mystery meteor" was observed in Central New York State by multiple witnesses from Rome to Buffalo, an aerial distance of over 160 miles. One witness, a schoolteacher in Rochester, New York, said, "Its path was wider and more brilliant than lightning, and it traveled at great speed. It was very beautiful and brilliant. The street was like day for fully two minutes. There was no sound."

The *Democrat and Chronicle* of Rochester, in its April 8, 1906 edition, said experts agreed the aerial

EARLY 20th CENTURY UFOs

object was not "lightning, or a shooting star, or some other ordinary, every-day thing." The head of the U.S. Weather Bureau in Rochester, Mr. L. M. Dey, was so intrigued by the object that he "aroused the interest of the scientists in the service of the bureau" to investigate the mysterious object.

Rochester, NY, in 1909 (Library of Congress)

Within three weeks of the event, Dey had received close to twenty letters from eyewitnesses, each telling their version of what they saw. He was particularly struck by the fact that all accounts seemed to agree that at the end of the sighting, the object merely "vanished." Dey felt that the object had burned itself up in its rapid flight through the Earth's atmosphere, although other explanations for its sudden disappearance were posed by others.

From his office at the Weather Bureau, Dey made a concerted effort to gather as much data as possible about this unusual event. The newspapers reported, "Mr. Dey is exceedingly desirous of collecting reliable data from those who had a good view of the meteor. He asks especially that observers in writing their descriptions give the apparent angular attitude and bearings of the

AMERICAN SIGHTINGS: 1900-1919

meteor, as seen by them. He doesn't want hearsay or second-hand information but wants descriptions from persons who actually saw the meteor."

> ## Wants All the Meteor Data That Veracious Observers Can Supply
>
> **Has Received Score of Letters, but Wants to Hear From More People Who Saw the Phenomenon.**
>
> Persons who insisted on telling their friends on the morning of March 15th of the brilliant meteor that flashed through the heavens the evening before, and who were pooh-poohed, with the explanation that it was lightning, or a shooting star, or some other ordinary, every-day thing, are to have their revenge.
>
> The literature of astronomy is to be enriched by an account of an official investigation of Rochester's great meteor, and due credence will be given to the statements of reliable persons who observed the phenomenon. L. M. Dey, head of the Rochester branch of the Weather Bureau, has aroused the interest of the scientists in the service of the bureau.
>
> There is no doubt that the phenomenon was generally observed. In Rochester dozens of persons spoke of it for days afterward. Mr. Vanderpool, the forecast official, received the next day a letter from a little girl, who, with her childish credulity, looked upon the brilliant illumination as an answer to her prayer that the streets would be sufficiently light to enable her to do an errand without being afraid.
>
> A school teacher in Rochester, who was in Orange street on the night of the illumination, had an excellent view.
>
> "It seemed more like lightning than any other thing I can compare it to," she said. "Its path was wider and more brilliant than lightning, and it traveled at great speed. It was very beautiful and brilliant. The street was like day for fully two minutes. There was no sound. I never quite understood what speed really meant until I saw the way that meteor traveled through the sky."
>
> The phenomenon was observed as far east as Syracuse and as far west as Medina. Mr. Dey has received nearly twenty letters bearing upon the meteor, all giving accounts of its passage. While there is a wide difference of opinion among the observers as to the size of the meteor, all agree that it vanished suddenly. Mr. Dey believes that when the meteor "vanished" it ceased to exist, having burned up in its rapid flight through the earth's atmosphere.
>
> Mr. Dey is exceedingly desirous of collecting reliable data from those who had a good view of the meteor. He asks especially that observers in writing their descriptions give the apparent angular attitude and bearings of the meteor, as seen by them. He doesn't want hearsay or second-hand information, but wants descriptions from persons who actually saw the meteor. Information should be sent to Mr. Dey at his offices in the Federal building.
>
> *Democrat and Chronicle (Rochester, New York), Apr. 8, 1906, p. 24*

Writing a year later, in the March 1907 edition of the *Monthly Weather Review*, astronomy professor Henry A. Peck, PhD of Syracuse University gave his opinion that the mysterious meteor "was a remarkable object from a popular as well as from a scientific standpoint."

EARLY 20th CENTURY UFOs

> **THE METEOR OF MARCH 14, 1906, OVER CENTRAL NEW YORK.**
> By Prof. HENRY A. PECK. Dated Syracuse University, Syracuse, N. Y., May 1, 1907.
>
> About 8 p. m., March 14, 1906, a large meteor past over the western-central part of New York State. Press notices appeared in the majority of the daily papers between Rome and Buffalo. In an attempt to secure more reliable data requests were sent from the Central Office of the Weather Bureau to the officials in charge at Oswego, Ithaca, Syracuse, and Rochester, asking them to send all good accounts of the meteor, together with apparent angular altitudes and bearings. Scattering observations were obtained from the three first named stations. In response to advertisements in the Rochester papers, Mr. L. M. Dey, the local forecaster, was enabled to obtain a large amount of material which has been of great value in roughly outlining the territory over which the meteor was observed, as well as in determining the general character of the phenomenon. A complete list of those who have contributed to secure the following result is here given, the places of observation being arranged in order of longitude west of Greenwich:
>
> Henry B. French, Rome.
> J. W. Blood, Rome.
> L. W. Griswold, Oneida.
> H. A. Peck, Syracuse.
> Jennie Whaley, Oswego.
> Olive E. Templeton, Oswego.
> F. B. Monk, Fair Haven.
> S. D. Colgate, Townsendville.
> Benjamin Christian, Wolcott.
> F. W. Clark, Williamson.
> Rev. J. Monlendyke, Palmyra.
> J. Van Arsdale, Canandaigua.
> Mrs. Addie Eddy, Middlesex.
> C. D. Gilbert, Despatch.
> B. D. Pilcopton, Victor.
> Mrs. Jesse A. Wheeler, Holcomb.
> Benjamin G. Wedd, Mortimer.
> William B. Mason, Lima.
> Jesse L. Vanderpool, Rochester.
> L. M. Dey, Rochester.
> F. L. Hunt, Rochester.
> Kate E. Collins, Rochester.
> Julia F. White, Rochester.
> H. B. McEntee, Rochester.
> Mrs. T. Tewilliger, Rochester.
> Mrs. F. B. Allero, Rochester.
> Mrs. Chas. T. Axelson, Rochester.
> Mrs. George Holverling, Rochester.
> Adaline I. Jones, Rochester.
> Katherine L. Hoyt, Rochester.
> Mrs. O. T. Le Beuillier, Rochester.
> Robert J. Purdy, Ovid.
> Floyd Thomas, North Rose.
> Louis H. Albright, Rochester.
> J. A. Ross, Lyons.
> O. J. Andrews, Sodus Center.
> Fred Webber, Sodus Center.
> Professor Le Roy, Penn Yan.
> Oliver R. Tobey, Penn Yan.
> V. C. Washburn, Clifton Springs.
> P. T. Ellison, Rochester.
> S. P. Gould, Rochester.
> A. E. Benjamin, Rochester.
> Edgar Shantz, Rochester.
> C. J. Trumater, Rochester.
> Louis P. Hof, Rochester.
> F. W. Green, Rochester.
> H. B. Butler, Rochester.
> Frank J. Schantz, Rochester.
> Milton J. Tripp, Rochester.
> Mrs. H. H. Turner, Rochester.
> S. L. Pope, Rochester.
> Lerean Gibbs, Livonia Center.
> George V. Witzel, Goldwater.
> F. Hanford, Scottsville.
> W. J. Stocum, Athens Basin.
> John Deaton, M. D., Retsof.
> Ames Beldon, Albion.
> Georgianna A. Nichol, Medina.
> Mrs. Thomas B. Griffith, Aurora.
> Thomas Rooney, Lockport.
> F. A. Kellinger, M. D., Lockport.
>
> When it is remembered that the air-line distance from Rome to Lockport is over 160 miles, it is evident that the meteor was a remarkable object from a popular as well as from a scientific standpoint.
>
> The apparent path of the meteor thru the atmosphere began about 4 miles to the southeast of Geneva, on the eastern shore of Seneca Lake, at an altitude of 70 miles above the surface of the earth. The time of flight was about five or six seconds, and it disappeared over Lake Ontario northeast of Manitou Point, about 8 miles from the nearest land. At first it appeared as a rosy red star of not inconsiderable brightness, but in the latter part of its flight various observers estimated its size as from that of quarter to the full size of the moon. The light cast at places near its path was evidently as strong as that of the moon, or, as one observer says, "the beam of a strong searchlight". Some doubt might be cast on its having been one large, solid body from the fact that reports from places widely apart state that fragments seemed to leave the main mass and pursue separate paths. As suggested by Mr. L. M. Dey, official in charge of the Weather Bureau office at Rochester, this may be the cause of some of the conflicting accounts as to the course, some observers having seen fragments of the parent body. A trail that persisted for several seconds followed the flight. A number of observers report that it made a sound as of some heavy body rushing thru the air. After passing over Lake Ontario it exploded twice, the detonation being heard 40 miles, while within 25 miles the concussion was so great as to cause a slight shaking of houses. The sound at Rochester and vicinity is compared to the sound of distant cannon or blasting, or to the rolling of thunder.[1]
>
> To obtain the orbit of such an object, using as the basis the conflicting observations and estimates of persons who, for the most part, are unskilled in such work, is no easy task. It must be remembered in the present instance that the greater share of the accounts were not compiled from notes made at the time of observation, but were compiled from memory about three weeks later. Under such circumstances the observer will often unconsciously and in perfect good faith prolong the true path in either direction.
>
> Our work falls into two divisions. We must first find the most probable path thru the atmosphere, assuming that path as a straight line, from which, in any event, it can not deviate very materially during the short time of flight. The straight line is fixt if we know its length, and its direction. The known time of flight furnishes the velocity. The second
>
> [1] A great noise is sometimes heard shortly after a large meteor passes the observer, and as meteors are frequently seen to break into two or more portions such noises are spoken of as concussions or explosions, especially because they are so loud as to resemble cannonading. However there is generally no explosion, properly so called, even when the noises are very loud; and the exact mechanism by which the noises are produced is worthy of further study.—C. A.

Monthly Weather Review, March 1907, p. 121

Peck also said, "At first it appeared as a rosy red star of not inconsiderable brightness, but in the latter part of its flight various observers estimated its size as from that of quarter to the full size of the moon. The light cast at places near its path was evidently as strong as that of the moon, or as one observer says, 'the beam of a strong searchlight.'"

Peck also points out that the object may not have been a single, solitary object. "Reports from places widely apart state that fragments seemed to leave the main mass and pursue separate paths."

Peck also addressed the final "vanishing" of the object, stating, "After passing over Lake Ontario it exploded twice, the detonation being heard 40 miles, while within 25 miles the concussion was so

AMERICAN SIGHTINGS: 1900-1919

great as to cause a slight shaking of houses. The sound at Rochester and vicinity is compared to the sound of distant cannon or blasting, or to the rolling of thunder."

Rochester, NY, Circa 1906

In conclusion, the "mystery meteor" seen over the skies of Rochester on March 14, 1906 appears to have been something out of the ordinary. Its observed trajectory did not seem to be meteor-like. Its brightness, especially in the terms of the light it

EARLY 20th CENTURY UFOs

projected down to the ground below, also seemed beyond the normal. The many observers of this passing object all seemed to agree that it was unlike other instances of meteors that they had previously witnessed in years past. Was it even really a meteor? Paranormal researchers over the years have favored the view that it was something entirely different, namely an unidentified flying object.

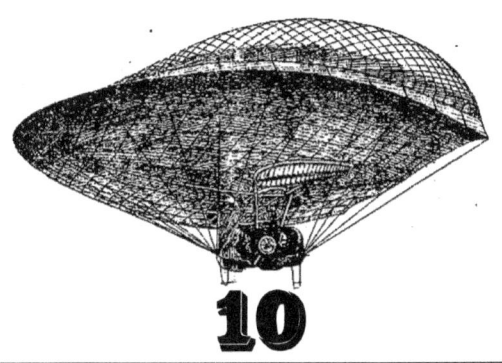

10
THE MAN WHO VISITED MARS
August 13, 1906
Syracuse, New York

A FASCINATING CHARACTER who invented a number of devices and was a strong believer in the paranormal, Sackville Gwyn Leyson (1854 - 1919) of Syracuse, New York, claimed that in August 1906, he traveled to the planet Mars and interacted with several life forms upon the planet. Although history has proven that wherever he really went, it was not Mars, Leyson's story is nonetheless fascinating and worthy of our attention, for its quirkiness if nothing else.

The report of Leyson's sensational, alleged trip to Mars was published in hundreds of major U.S. newspapers in August 1906, including the *Chicago (Illinois) Tribune* and the *New York Tribune.*

EARLY 20ᵗʰ CENTURY UFOs

The Planet Mars (European Space Agency)

Leyson was not the first psychic to claim the ability to travel to other planets by what is now known as either "astral projection" or "remote viewing." As noted in the second book of this series *Old West UFOs*, in 1867 Professor William Denton, a geologist of some note, and his family of Wellesley, Massachusetts, claimed to have traveled frequently to Mars in "spirit," while their physical bodies remained on Earth. Denton's method was more akin to what we call "remote viewing," in that he believed that merely focusing on a planet in the night sky would enable a person to travel there by remote.

AMERICAN SIGHTINGS: 1900-1919

SEES MARS; TALE AMAZES.

CHIEF PSYCHIC BRINGS BACK A QUEER ACCOUNT OF PLANET.

Sackville G. Leyson of Syracuse, N. Y., Declares He Journeyed 141,-000,000 Miles in Forty Minutes to Earth's Nearest Terrestrial Neighbor and There Saw One Eyed Giants with Noses Like Lions and Pygmies That Could Walk Up a Wall.

Syracuse, N. Y., Aug 13.—[Special.]—Sackville G. Leyson, president of the Society for Psychical Research, says he recently paid a visit to Mars. Although the distance is 141,-000,000 miles, his spirit went there and back in forty minutes while his body lay in his residence. In describing his visit he said:

"When I approached Mars it looked like a big globe of fire, and it seemed as if I were about to plunge into a molten mass. It was surrounded by blood red clouds mixed with others of greenish hue.

Martians Like Elephants and Ants.

"There are two tribes of people on Mars—one so large I only came up to their knees and the other so small that they only came up to my knees. None wore clothing. All were covered with hair.

"The larger species had huge ears, a nose like a lion, and only one eye, in the middle of the forehead. Their lungs do not move up and down in breathing, but expand crosswise.

Walk Right Up the Wall.

"The little men lived in holes in the ground or rocks. The larger ones had houses made of rocks. The little ones had web feet and slipped over a mosslike substance as though skating. They could walk up perpendicular walls like flies.

"The small ones have two eyes, one in each temple. They had no noses, but there was a hole in each cheek.

"The trees looked as if made of rubber. I saw none decayed. There was a substance which looked like snow, but which was not cold and was easy and soft to walk on.

"Down in a deep chasm I saw men working with some sort of machines which were guiding lights across transparent rocks. The rays seemed to be reflected clear to the atmosphere of earth."

Chicago Tribune, Aug. 14, 1906, p. 2

Leyson, on the other hand, apparently employed some psychic method that supposedly separated his "spirit" from his physical body and projected his spirit to the other world, in this case Mars. Leyson described a harrowing trip through space and his final approach to Mars, "When I approached Mars, it looked like a big globe of fire and it seemed as though I were about to plunge into a molten mass. It was surrounded blood red clouds, mixed with others of greenish hue."

Six years after Leyson supposedly projected himself onto the surface of Mars, the same method of space travel was featured in the novel *A Princess of Mars*, written by Edgar Rice Burroughs, who also wrote the Tarzan novels. It is unknown whether Burroughs was inspired by the alleged Mars voyages of either the Sackville Leyson or William Denton; however, there are some vague similarities between the Mars described by these two men and the Mars described in *A Princess of Mars*.

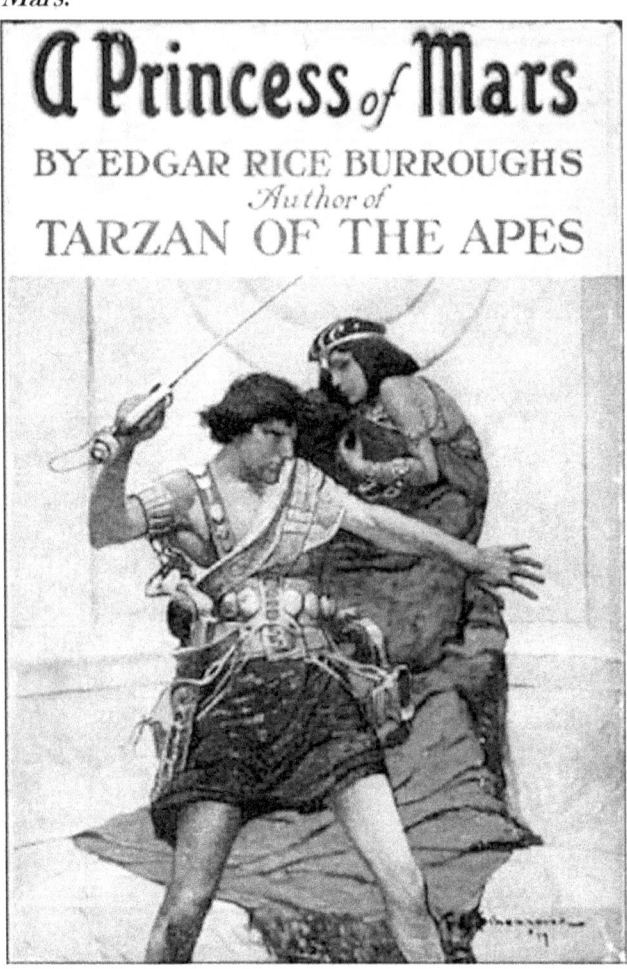

Although Leyson achieved considerable national attention in 1906, a lot of the media coverage seemed quite tongue-in-cheek. One report said, "Sackville G. Leyson ... recently paid a visit to

AMERICAN SIGHTINGS: 1900-1919

Mars, and although the distance is 111 million miles, he says he went there and back in forty minutes - at least his spirit did, while his body was in his residence at 131 South Avenue."

The planet Mars - now known to be desert-like, forbidding, and void of any life - was described by Leyson as teaming with all manner of life, including several very odd species of humanoid beings. Leyson told reporters, "There are two tribes of people on Mars, one so large I only came up to their knees, and the other so small that they only came up to my knees. None wore clothing, and all were covered with hair."

He added, "The larger species had huge ears and a nose like a lion and only one eye in the middle of the forehead. Their lungs do not move up and down in breathing, but expand crosswise."

The Tracks of NASA's Mars Curiosity Rover are Seen as it Explores the Planet's Desolate Landscape (NASA - 2014)

EARLY 20th CENTURY UFOs

Whatever place Leyson visited in his mind was definitely not the planet Mars. His description of the Martians included the following: "The little men lived in holes in the ground or rocks. The larger ones had houses made of stones. The little ones had web feet and slipped over a moss-like substance as if skating. They could walk up perpendicular walls like flies. The small ones have two eyes, one in each temple. They had no nose but there was a hole in each cheek."

Syracuse Man Says He Visited the Planet.

[By Telegraph to The Tribune.]

Syracuse, Aug. 13.—Sackville G. Leyson, of this city, who has been a student of the occult, says that he recently took a trip to Mars while in a trance, and says he is ready to do the same thing again before an audience of scientists. He leaves his body behind, and only his spirit goes through space. In describing two wonderful races of men he found in Mars he says:

"One race was so large that I only came to their knees, while another only came to my knees. None wore clothing, and all were covered with hair. The large species had huge ears, a nose like a lion and only one eye in the middle of the forehead. The little men had web feet and lived in holes in the ground, while the large ones lived in houses built of rocks. The little ones could walk up perpendicular walls, as if they were flies. They had no nose, but there was a hole in each cheek.

"Everything seemed to be made in a serpentine form, even the roads. Through the equatorial belt of the planet was a wide belt of water, probably nine miles across. Some of the animals were green. I saw many of the big men working with a big machine, which cast light on to transparent rocks, reflecting it far into space and nearly to the atmosphere of the earth. When I approached Mars it looked like a ball of fire."

New-York Tribune, Aug. 14, 1906, p. 1

AMERICAN SIGHTINGS: 1900-1919

While such imaginative descriptions of non-human entities may have thrilled Leyson's audiences and sold thousands of newspapers, they clearly had no basis in reality whatsoever.

"The trees looked as if made of rubber," Leyson said, "I saw none decayed. There was a substance which looked like snow, but which was not cold and was easy to walk on. Down in a deep chasm, I saw men working with some sort of machines which were guiding lights across transparent rocks and the rays seemed to be reflected clear to the atmosphere of the earth."

In the *New York Tribune*, Leyson was quoted as saying "Everything seemed to be made in a serpentine form, even the roads. Through the equatorial belt of the planet was a wide belt of water, probably nine miles across. Some of the animals were green."

The various articles about Leyson concluded by stating, "Leyson says he will go to Mars again when he has an audience of scientists and psychologists to testify to the truth of his statement." After this, no further mention of Leyson or any future journeys to Mars could be found in the historical record.

However, a day or two later, the *St. Louis (Missouri) Post-Dispatch* reported that a woman in New York had, six years earlier, received a visit from a giant one-eyed Martian, which she felt confirmed the story that Leyson had told of his voyage to Mars and what he witnessed there.

Paulinet Corri, 66, said in a letter that she had seen "a shadowy, gigantic figure covered with hair;

EARLY 20th CENTURY UFOs

not the hair that serves as coating for four-footed animals, but soft and silky in texture and light in color." She added, "The figure had but one eye, and that was in the center of the forehead."

Then Corri claims she heard a voice from "somewhere" that stated to her, "He is a spirit from the planet Mars."

NEWS FROM MARS IS CONFIRMED

New York Woman Says She Had Visit From One-Eyed Giant Seen by Mr. Leyson.

By Leased Wire From the New York Bureau of the Post-Dispatch.

NEW YORK, Aug. 15.—There is a good deal of travel between the Earth and Mars, it seems. The Post-Dispatch yesterday published the account of his recent visit to Mars given by Sackville G. Leyson, president of the Society for Psychical Research of Syracuse, N. Y., whose spirit went to Mars and back, 141,000,000 miles, while his body remained in Syracuse.

Last night the Post-Dispatch bureau here received this letter from Paulinet Corri, 66 Irving place, New York:

"Because of an experience I had in London some six years ago I was considerably surprised when I read Mr. Leyson's account of his psychic visit to the planet Mars.

"I was busy at my desk when I became conscious of a strange presence, and looking up, saw a shadowy, gigantic figure covered with hair, not the hair that serves as coating for four-footed animals, but soft and silky in texture and light in color. The figure had but one eye, and that was in the center of the forehead.

"Naturally I was taken aback, awed. That my visitor was not flesh and blood I knew, and while I waited, with my flesh creeping, I heard from somewhere, but not the man, 'He is a spirit from the planet Mars.'

"That was all. He vanished and never returned, but this morning the vision recurred to my mind, and I wondered."

St. Louis (Missouri) Post-Dispatch, Aug. 15, 1906, p. 5

Interestingly, nothing further was heard of Leyson's supposed space traveling abilities. Some researchers have questioned if Sackville G. Leyson even existed and accused the newspaper reporters of fabricating him and the whole Martian narrative. However, our research shows that a real person by that name did exist, and his name appears on several patents filed with the U.S. government.

Interestingly, his patent applications run the gamut from medical devices to an electric animal trap. If this inventor was the same Sackville G. Leyson that claimed he traveled to Mars, it seems

AMERICAN SIGHTINGS: 1900-1919

likely that he was quite intelligent and possibly a genius.

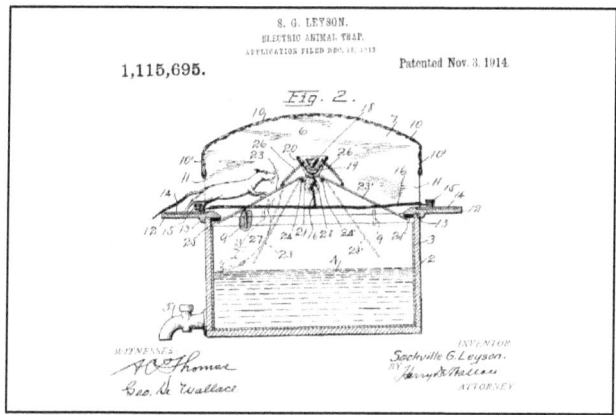

One of Several Patent Applications Filed by Sackville G. Leyson

As one final piece of evidence that Leyson really existed, there is a tombstone bearing his name at the Myrtle Hill Cemetery in Westvale, Onondaga County, New York. It gives his year of birth as 1854 and his year of death as 1919.

What exactly is to be made of Leyson's psychic experiences that he interpreted as a trip to Mars? What forces might have been at work on his mind to cause such a vision? We are left with many questions but few answers

EARLY 20th CENTURY UFOs

Returning to the subject of flying saucers, Mrs. DeMott says she never saw one.

"I was in one," says DeMott, "when I was about 10 years old, which would make it long before all the saucer sightings were reported."

He says the saucer came down near their water well in Mitchell, S.D.

"As I approached it," he adds, "a door rolled back and I was welcomed inside. Its two occupants sat inside on camp stools."

He says as he entered he saw a lever on the left and that the occupants looked like earthlings. They conversed with him fluently, but he didn't know where they came from, he says.

"The outer shell of the saucer was filled with helium gas, and when the lever was moved the magnetism from the earth was cut off, allowing the saucer to rise," says DeMott.

He says the saucer's occupants dipped water from the farm's horse trough to be used in making electricity.

DeMott says he has not seen a flying saucer since that time.

Albany (Oregon) Democrat-Herald, Aug. 27, 1973, p. 11

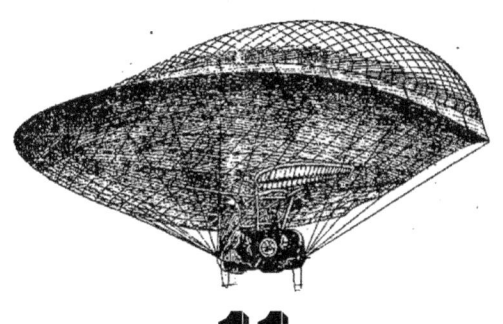

11
THE AIRSHIPS OF 1906

August - October 1906
South Dakota, Indiana, and
Oklahoma

BY 1906, IT HAD BEEN ten years since the first great airship wave. Certainly, strange things were still being seen in the sky, but not with the same frequency that they had during 1896 and 1897. After ten years of relative inactivity, suddenly airships seemed to reappear around North America, albeit on a smaller scale and with fewer impressive cases. What unfinished business caused them to come back? Where were they in the interim? Or, could it be, as some people suggest, that the nation's newspapermen attempted to resurrect the excitement of the airship craze in order to sell more papers? In this chapter, we will

EARLY 20th CENTURY UFOs

look at three of the most significant of the 1906 airship sightings.

The first case happened in Mitchell, South Dakota, in 1906, but it did not come to public light until published in the *Albany (Oregon) Democrat-Herald* on August 27, 1973, when it was disclosed to a reporter by the then 67-year-old eyewitness, Herbert Vern Demott. Back in 1906, Demott was ten years old and living on his family's South Dakota ranch, when he saw a "saucer" come down near a nearby water well.

Upon the craft's landing, young Demott approached the strange ship. As he did, a door "rolled back" and he was "welcomed inside." He described the two occupants as looking like "earthlings," and they "sat on camp stools" inside the ship. Though they engaged him in conversation, they never said who they were or where they came from, and apparently Demott did not think to ask.

As far as the flying ship, Demott seemed to grasp the basic mechanism that allowed it to lift off the ground and fly. He told the Albany newspaper, "The outer shell of the saucer was filled with helium gas, and when the lever was moved, the magnetism from the earth was cut off, allowing the saucer to rise."

The only other details he gave of the sighting was that the men drew water from a nearby horse trough to "be used in making electricity." Unfortunately, Demott died on Friday, March 8, 1974, just slightly more than six months after he disclosed his UFO sighting.

AMERICAN SIGHTINGS: 1900-1919

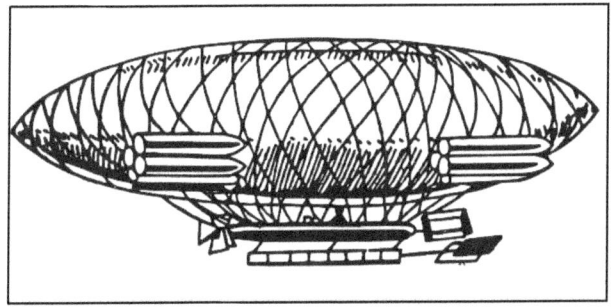

The next sighting was recorded by a retired soldier, John Warner, in Orinoco, Indiana. He was sitting on his back porch on the night of August 26, 1906, when he heard his horse making a strange noise in his barn. The sound was strange enough that he got up to check on the horse to see if it might be sick. The horse appeared to be fine, but as he walked back to his home, he heard a strange, rushing noise above.

He looked above to see a cigar-shaped airship. This one was painted green and had green lights. The airship touched down in his yard and out of it exited four normal-looking men. The article, which is rather brief, states that "[The men] informed [Warner] they were on their way to New York, from Chicago, and asked him which direction to take. He directed them as far as Seymour, when they turned on their power and sailed away." This was reported in the August 31st edition of the *Rockport Journal* out of Indiana.

A somewhat different version of the story, with the reporter's cynicism liberally added, appeared in the August 18, 1906 edition of the *Columbus (Indiana) Republic*. The writer of the story, with obvious tongue in cheek, suggests that the eyewitness is "the most truthful man in the county, next to George Washington." The reporter also makes the claim that although John Warner did not know the men on the airship, they knew him!

> ### Saw an Airship.
> John Warner, who lives in Orinoco, and who is the most truthful man in the county, next to George Washington, says he saw an airship last night. He was sitting on the back porch in his sock feet listening to the tune of the potato bug as he rubbed his wings against the fence, when an airship dropped low over his garden. He says he did not know the occupants of the ship but they know him, and asked him the way to New York. He directed them as far as Jonesville and they left in a hurry. Mr. Warner says the ship was painted green and carried green lights.
>
> *The Republic (Columbus, Indiana)*
> *Aug. 18, 1906, p. 5*

The third and final significant airship sighting of 1906 occurred in Oklahoma on a late October evening.

"A phenomenon of unusual nature is said to have been seen in the skies in Vincennes recently," began the article published in the November 9th edition of the *Bedford (Indiana) Weekly Mail.* The

AMERICAN SIGHTINGS: 1900-1919

article continued, "The moon was the cause of it all. The phenomenon according to the witnesses occurred on two different nights and for a time frightened those who saw it."

The witnesses included a Reverend Everett and his wife (her name not given, which is common of the time). Along with them were a Mr. John Potter and his wife and child, who were visiting Indiana from Oklahoma.

The reverend had been conducting a revival at the Oklahoma Baptist Church for several weeks. One night, on his way home to the Porter residence where he was staying, "he noticed that the moon seemed to break to pieces and then suddenly went back into its old position and was as bright as ever."

UFO researchers would argue that the witnesses were not observing the moon at all, but rather a bright, orb-like craft that they mistook to be the moon. The article continues that initially the witnesses said nothing of the strange sight until they witnessed it again. "One night this week, in company with his wife and Mr. and Mrs. Potter and their son, while again returning home from services they noticed that the moon again seemed to break apart and the image of a man was plainly visible. This lasted for two seconds and was seen by all five of the people. The image then disappeared and the moon went back to its old position and shone very brightly."

As this sighting in no way resembled a traditional airship (which the witnesses may have been aware of thanks to newspaper reports), the witnesses would not have thought to have interpreted it as

EARLY 20ᵗʰ CENTURY UFOs

such. Remember, the "airships" of the time were usually mysterious dirigibles. This was much more in line with a traditional UFO, which at the time were usually interpreted to be meteorological phenomena or "signs and wonders." This sighting was interpreted in the latter category, with the article concluding that, "The minister and the others are of the opinion that the warning was a herald of some approaching catastrophe. No one else as far as is known saw the warning."

SAW MOON BREAK

Rev. Everett, Of Washington, And Party Saw Strange Phenomenon At Vincennes.

A phenomenon of unusual nature is said to have been seen in the skies in Vincennes recently. The moon was the cause of it all. The phenomenon according to the witnesses occurred on two different nights and for a time frightened those who saw it. Rev. Everett and wife of Washington, Ind., John Potter and wife and child, who live in Oklahoma, were the witnesses to the thing, whatever it might have been.

Rev. Everett is conducting a revival at the Oklahoma Baptist church and has been in the city for several weeks. One night according to his story while returning home from church to the residence of John Potter where he resides while there, he noticed that the moon seemed to break to pieces and then suddenly went back into its old position and was as bright as ever. He said nothing of the matter but one night this week, in company with his wife and Mr. and Mrs. Potter and their son, while again returning home from services they noticed that the moon again seemed to break apart and the image of a man was plainly visible. This lasted for two seconds and was seen by all five of the people. The image then disappeared and the moon went back to its old position and shone very brightly.

The minister and the others are of the opinion that the warning was a herald of some approaching catastrophe. No one else as far as is known saw the warning.

The Bedford (Indiana) Weekly Mail, Nov. 6, 1906, p. 4

As these three sightings indicate, 1906 was "small potatoes" compared to the rash of sightings that occurred in 1896 and 1897. Still, it's intriguing to note that airship sightings made a bit of a comeback ten years after they had appeared to run their course. And interestingly, these three incidents heralded an even stranger airship story to come the following year, in 1907.

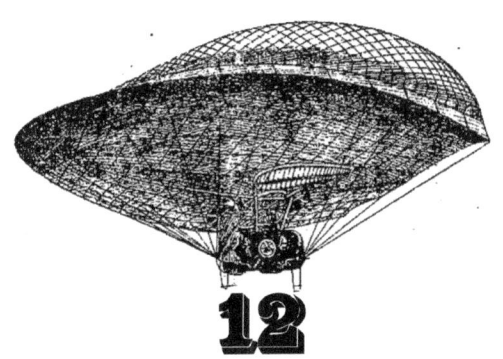

MUSIC OF THE AIRSHIPS
April 20-28, 1907
Tennessee

FOR ONE WEEK in late April, Tennessee was the theater for several of the more unique airship encounters of the early 20th century. It all began near Dikeman Springs, in the vicinity of Dickson, Tennessee, on the afternoon of Friday, April 19, 1907. The local newspaper said, "Walter Stephenson while out training a pair of bloodhounds near the Dikeman springs was subjected to a unique experience." A unique experience is an understatement.

Stephenson had just finished a long chase with his dogs when he sat down on a log to rest. "He

EARLY 20th CENTURY UFOs

espied upon the eastern horizon a speck, which he took to be a large kite. He paid little attention to the object, and shifted his gaze temporarily to other scenes." But then, as in so many other UFO encounters, Stephenson heard strange "whirring noises" and looked up to the sky to see "that the speck which he had a few moments before discovered in the eastern sky had approached almost directly over him, and that the object was in reality a huge balloon, but of a pattern and appearance he had never in his life before seen."

Clearly, this was no ordinary balloon, and it would soon begin to display other worldly behavior. As the "floating mass" rapidly approached the Earth, Stephens began to hear "strains of music calculated to charm." Suddenly, curious "spheres burst forth from the balloon!" These spheres "circled around and around" until they finally landed at Dikeman Springs. "A number of strange people emerged from the car," says the article. Stephens thought the beings seemed "angelic," glistening with a strange substance whenever "the sunshine that temporarily burst through the obscuring clouds" shone upon them. The strangers traveled down to the "big, flowing spring," and then "knelt by it in a supplicating attitude and so remained for a minute or more."

Stephenson sat quietly and watched the visitors rise to their feet. Supposing that "their devotional exercises were over, he asked if he might be permitted to inquire who they were, and what their mission?"

AMERICAN SIGHTINGS: 1900-1919

The next detail is interesting, as it implies these beings were wearing odd garments. Upon hearing Stephenson's question, one of the beings lifted a visor to reveal "the benign face of a lady." The woman then asked him, "Haben sie Beten?" As it turned out she was speaking German and asked him, "Did you pray?"

> **WIERD TALE FROM DICKSON**
>
> Queer Brand of Liquor Must Be Used in That Country.
>
> DICKSON, Tenn. April 20 (Special) — Walter Stephenson while out hunting a pair of bloodhounds near the Dickman spring to-day, was subjected to a unique experience. He had just finished a long chase with his dogs and sat down on a log to rest, when he espied upon the eastern horizon a speck, which he took to be a large kite. He paid but little attention to the object and shifted his gaze temporarily to other scenes. Soon his attention was attracted to a whirring noise and looking upward he saw that the speck which he had a few moments before discovered in the eastern sky had approached almost directly over him, and that the object was in reality a huge balloon, but of a pattern and appearance he had never in his life before seen. He discovered that the floating mass was rapidly approaching the earth. Of a sudden the observer says strains of music calculated to charm the spheres burst from the balloon which circled round and round and finally landed at the Dikeman Spring. A number of strange looking people emerged from the car which was closely curtained with a substance that fairly glistened in the sunshine that temporarily burst through the obscuring clouds, and all going to the big, flowing spring knelt by it in a supplicating attitude and so remained for a minute or more. Mr. Stephenson says that while this was going on he sat quietly within speaking distance, and when the strange visitors arose to their feet and he supposed their devotional exercises was over, he asked if he might be permitted to inquire who they were, and what their mission? He says that instantly a visard was lifted by one of the company and the benign face of a lady showed from underneath and said in German, "Haben sie Beten?" (did you pray?)" and instantly all were aboard, the air ship rose, circled about for a minute or more and was gone in a westerly direction.
>
> Mr. Stephenson says that the incident left an impression upon him that he can never forget, and while he knows that it was some human invention, it looked and the music sounded, more like that of angels than of mortals
>
> *The Nashville (Tennessee) American, Apr. 21, p. 21*

Upon asking the question, the woman and her companions magically returned to the airship: "And instantly all were aboard, the airship rose, circled about for a minute or more and was gone in a westerly direction."

The article concludes, "Mr. Stephenson says that the incident left an impression upon him that he can never forget, and while he knows that it was

EARLY 20th CENTURY UFOs

some human invention, it looked and the music sounded more like that 'of angels than of mortals.'" Stephenson contended that, although the craft looked manmade, its bizarre occupants seemed to be not of this earth. If the beings were indeed aliens rather than angels, then UFO researchers would certainly classify them as belonging to the "Nordic" type of extraterrestrial. The Nordics often appear benevolent and are usually physically attractive.

That the "aliens" spoke German is interesting, and apparently Stephenson was of German descent, because he understood the language spoken to him by the visitors.

Another sighting was reported the very next day on April 20th in Bold Springs, Tennessee at 3:30 a.m. on Saturday morning. Remember, Stephenson's story from Friday would not yet have been reported by the time the witness, Mr. W. A. Smith, "a respected farmer living four miles from the town of Bold Springs", had his sighting. Or, in other words, Smith was unlikely to have been influenced by Stephenson's sighting as the article about Stephenson was not published until the following day, April 21.

Smith was riding along the road that early morning when he heard strange music. Smith thought that perhaps a wedding had lasted late into the night. Why else would music be heard at 3:30 in the morning?

But when Smith looked into the sky, he was shocked to see "a large balloon of unusual size and strange pattern." A car hung from beneath the balloon, and the music seemed to be coming from there. Electric lights were strung all about the car, and from the front end shone a bright searchlight. Smith could see no machinery or mechanism that propelled the strange craft.

Again, the balloon was drawn towards a large spring, which it shown its searchlight upon and drifted towards. Smith watched as the balloon slowly descended to the spring.

KNEEL IN PRAYER BESIDE SPRING

HUMPHREYS COUNTY MAN LOCATES NEW BRAND OF DOPE AND SEES THINGS.

BOLD SPRINGS, Tenn., April 21.—(Special.)—W. A. Smith, a respected farmer living four miles from town, comes to the front with a story that, but for Mr. Smith's reputation, would probably be received with incredulity. Mr. Smith tells his story with bated breath, and it can be readily seen that he has passed through an experience which has left a deep impression upon him.

Having occasion to come to town Saturday morning, Mr. Smith left home about 2:30 o'clock. He had proceeded but a little distance when he heard strains of music, but paid little attention, the sound being afar off, and Mr. Smith judging that some darky wedding or other festivity was being unusually prolonged.

A few moments later, however, he was suddenly impressed with the fact that the strains, while no louder than he had at first heard, appeared to come from above rather than from a horizontal direction. He looked up and was amazed to see a large balloon of unusual size and strange pattern, suspended from the balloon was a large closed car from within which the music appeared to come. The car was strung with electric lights, and a brilliant searchlight was carried at the front. No machinery or mechanism appeared in view, and the motive power could not even be surmised.

Near the spot where Mr. Smith saw the balloon is a large spring, and the searchlight, as Mr. Smith recalled later, was trained upon this spring. The car appeared to be headed directly towards it, and finally the balloon dropped slowly and almost tenderly to the ground, landing possibly thirty feet from the edge of the spring.

Mr. Smith, although startled and surprised beyond measure, was not timorous, and he whipped up his horse at the first sight of the balloon, and managed to be close by when the balloon alighted. He left his horse tied to a tree by the roadside and approached the spring. As he came closer he noted a peculiar party of queer-looking persons in strange garb kneeling beside the spring, apparently engaged in silent prayer. Mr. Smith wondered greatly at the unusual spectacle, but did not "butt in." The party returned to the car without partaking of the waters of the spring, and as they were boarding their aerial craft one of them pointed to Mr. Smith, who was not as well concealed as he had imagined. This discoverer of Mr. Smith uttered something, the words being, however, foreign and unintelligible to Mr. Smith.

Mr. Smith's narrative stops here. When asked what direction the strange craft had taken, or whether any of the others had replied to the remarks of the first who had spoken, Mr. Smith answered that he didn't know. "I decided it was late and that I had better hurry to town," he said. "And I left."

In justice to Mr. Smith, it should be stated that his story was told here Saturday afternoon, nearly sixteen hours before The Sunday American reached town. In Sunday's American appeared a story from Jackson, Tenn., in the adjoining county, chronicling the appearance of a similar air craft, and crediting the strange visitors with speaking German.

The Nashville (Tenn.) American, April 22, 1907, p. 2

EARLY 20th CENTURY UFOs

Smith tied his horse to a tree and walked towards the craft. Like Stephenson before him, he saw people in strange clothing kneeling by the spring. Like Stephenson, he presumed them to be praying. But, unlike the previous witness, Smith was too timid to make contact. However, as the beings returned to their craft, one pointed to him and uttered something in a language that he could not understand. Perhaps it was again German?

The *Nashville American* wished to assure readers that Smith was not copying Stephenson, and closed their article by stating: "In justice to Mr. Smith it should be stated that his story was told here Saturday afternoon, nearly 16 hours before the Sunday *American* reached town. In Sunday's *American* appeared a story from Dickson, Tenn., in the adjoining county, chronicling the appearance of a similar aircraft, and crediting the strange visitors with speaking German."

On April 23rd, the *Nashville American* reported on yet another sighting, this one in the vicinity of Pleasant Spring, Tennessee. On the evening of the 21st, German immigrant Herman Schubert, also saw the visitors. As Schubert was a German, he confirmed that the aliens were indeed speaking his language and he regarded them as "visitors from the old country."

Schubert and his family lived on the edge of town on a large farm that contained, what else, a large spring! Sunday evening Schubert was finishing the day's work when he heard his 15-year old son, Carl, call out to him. Schubert ran out to see what his son was calling to him for. Several hundred feet

AMERICAN SIGHTINGS: 1900-1919

into the air he saw a large airship that looked similar to a balloon. The description was consistent with that of the previous two witnesses, complete with the enclosed car that hung from the craft. Schubert described the car as similar to a stage coach, only larger at 35 feet long with entrances at both sides.

AERONAUTS AT PLEASANT SPRING

MYSTERIOUS GERMAN AIR TRAVELERS ENCOUNTERED BY FARMER AND HIS SON.

The Nashville American (Nashville, Tenn.) April 23, 1907, p. 3

As the airship landed near the spring, Schubert and his son ran inside their springhouse to hide. Twelve to fourteen people [Schubert couldn't seem to decide on an exact number] exited the craft. Schubert said that the beings exuded an attitude of reverence towards the spring, "as though standing on sacred ground, or in a sacred presence."

As in the other recent encounters, the group knelt and prayed silently for several minutes. As the beings returned to the airship Schubert's curiosity got the best of him and he left the house to ask the people who they were and what they were doing.

EARLY 20th CENTURY UFOs

All but one ignored him, and turned to say, in German, "Thou has not prayed; address us not."

Unlike the experience of Mr. Stephenson, this being did not lift its visor to address to Schubert. Unlike Stephenson, Schubert was able to reply in German and ask them to elaborate. The being replied, "Our pilgrimage is not yet completed; the world will know all in time." The being returned to the ship with its companions, and the airship ascended swiftly and then took off to the south.

The comment that "the world will know all in time" is quite striking, especially in the context of what was happening in in Germany in 1913. What the world would soon "know" is that Germany instigated World War I just six years after this strange airship encounter. World War I resulted in an estimated 40 million deaths, and World War II, which stemmed from the first war and was also instigated by Germany, caused the deaths of as many as 80 million people. It was almost as if the strangers seen by Stephenson were imploring him to pray for the world, because two catastrophic world wars involving Germany were just on the horizon - wars that would kill off a significant part of the Earth's population (about 10 percent).

This possible reference to the upcoming world wars begs the question: Could the airship occupants have been time travelers? Would time travelers have been able to alter the inevitability of war?

The fourth and final sighting was reported in the *Nashville American* on April 28th. It was possibly the most fantastic of the encounters. This time the

AMERICAN SIGHTINGS: 1900-1919

witness was a mail carrier, Asa Hickerson, and the sighting took place near Nashville.

It was early in the morning while Hickerson was descending a steep hill on his way to the Peabody School. Suddenly he heard "sounds resembling the chanting of some weird, funeral dirge, proceeding seemingly from the tops of the forest trees through which his route winded." His horse became spooked as well, and so Hickerson dismounted his buggy to check on the animal when again he heard the strange noise, only louder.

Then he saw it, a large airship that flew into his line of sight with the grace and ease of a bird. It landed gently on the ground only 50 yards from him. Hickerson did his best to observe the craft while also steadying his panicked horse.

Hickerson observed several beings, which he identified as men, depart the same carrying car seen by all the other witnesses. In a single file, they walked towards the mouth of an abandoned oil well while chanting.

The group formed a circle around the well and an odd ritual commenced where one of them plunged a long staff into the well three times after having made "sundry passes in the air" with it. The beings then walked to the other side of the road with the staff, now dripping with oil. They stuck it into the earth and then lit it on fire. The group then began to sing and lifted their conjoined hands as they circled the flaming rod as smoke drifted into the air.

After the strange ritual finished, Hickerson asked the men what they had been doing. Once again,

EARLY 20th CENTURY UFOs

only one responded by extending his hand, and speaking in German, "Be healthy and pray." The huge airship then ascended into the air, never to be seen again.

On the surface, the story is encouraging because the witnesses all offer similar details that corroborate each other's stories. However, by the same token, all the stories were reported in the *Nashville American* and as such could have all been concocted by the same writer.

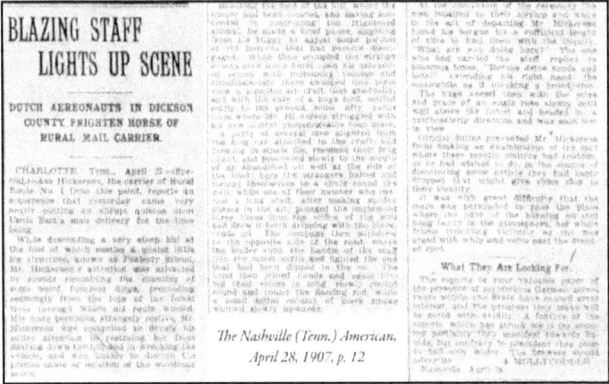

The Nashville (Tenn.) American, April 28, 1907, p. 12

The story's strangest detail isn't necessarily that all the beings spoke German, but that all but one of the witnesses were able to either understand what was said or repeat it verbatim to someone who could. For instance, if someone spoke to you in a foreign tongue, it could be very difficult to repeat what you heard. And yet, all but one of the witnesses managed to either repeat what they had heard, or understood it in person. Perhaps the areas had a high concentration of German immigrants?

AMERICAN SIGHTINGS: 1900-1919

BALLOON SAILS OVER THE CITY

Strange Aerial Craft Startles the Populace—Airship had Music and Beautiful Woman.

Residents in the lower end of town were amazed late yesterday afternoon by the sudden appearance of a balloon in the sky above the new bridge, at an apparent elevation of 800 or a thousand feet.

The strange craft was moving at a high rate of speed, borne swiftly along by a strong wind, and soon disappeared over the crest of Badger Mountain.

The sky craft was of the dirigible class, equipped with a long cigar-shaped gas bag, beneath which hung suspended what seemed to be a cabin with propelling mechanism.

The flight of the airship was so swift that but a fleeting glimpse of it was afforded the astonished spectators. Some of the more excited in the crowd claim that they distinctly heard strains of music issuing from the cabin of the sky craft.

According to a hunter who viewed the strange craft through field glasses from the crest of Saddle Rock three persons were visible upon the deck of the cabin, two men and a woman of rare beauty.

A fisherman who happened to be perched on a log just below the bridge when the balloon passed over, insists that a paper was tossed from the fleety flying craft, but that it unfortunately fell into the river and was carried away. If a man engaged in any other vocation than fishing had told this the statement would carry more weight with those interested in clearing up the mystery.

LATER: Special wireless to the Daily World:

OMAK, Sept. 17, 7 a. m.—A strange looking airship has just passed over the town, creating a profound sensation. It was headed northwest: thought to be Japanese war balloon. Superstitious Indians in panic-clamoring for whiskey to quiet their nerves. Town in an uproar. Send Bill Simmons at once.

The Wenatchee (Washington) Daily World, Sep. 17 1907, p. 1

The arcane fire ritual performed by these travelers relating to both fire and water is certainly puzzling. Could these have been time travelers on a strange mission? Perhaps they came from a time where water was scarce? Or, perhaps they were aliens from a planet where water was scarce. Or, maybe the darned reporter who wrote the articles for the Nashville American made it all up. We will likely never know.

The original researcher that unearthed these fascinating stories was Theo Paijmans, in his article "The Tennessee Aeronaut Flap of 1907."

Before we depart onto the next chapter, there was possibly one other sighting of the same airship

EARLY 20th CENTURY UFOs

we would like to discuss. Even better, it wasn't reported on by the *Nashville American*, and the sighting occurred in Wenatchee, Washington, on September 16, 1907, and was reported the next day in the *Wenatchee Daily World*.

Late in the afternoon, Wenatchee residents observed a dirigible flying at an elevation of 900 feet over a newly built bridge. The airship moved so swiftly that residents were barely able to observe it before it disappeared over Badger Mountain. Witnesses described the craft as having a long cigar-shaped gas bag, beneath which hung a car complete with some type of propelling mechanism. As in other recent cases, a few witnesses claimed to hear music coming from the car!

Luckily, a hunter was able to better observe the craft through his field glasses atop Saddle Rock. He claimed to have seen, within the car, two men and a "woman of rare beauty."

A fisherman that sat below the bridge when the airship flew over claimed that as it passed, a piece of paper was dropped from the craft. Perhaps this note contained the secrets "that the world will know all in time," as mentioned in the Pleasant Spring encounter. But we will never know, because, according to the fisherman, the note from the airship fluttered through the air and fell right into the river, sinking beneath the water.

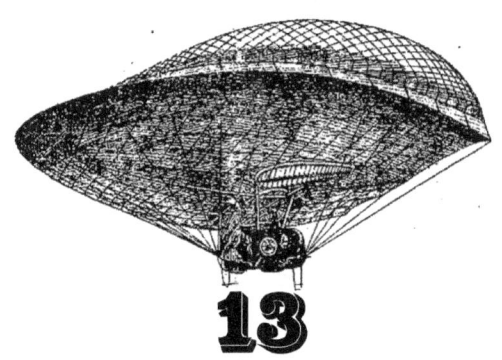

13
UFO EXPLOSION IN VERMONT
July 2, 1907
Burlington, Vermont

NEWSPAPER ACCOUNTS of the day said that what happened in Burlington, Vermont, on July 2, 1907, was a "remarkable celestial phenomenon." Today we would simply call it a close encounter with a UFO. It was witnessed by several of the leading men of the community, including John S. Michaud, the Roman Catholic Bishop of Burlington, and Urban A. Woodbury, former governor of Vermont.

On July 2 at about 11 a.m., a strange object appeared in downtown Burlington "along College street," according to Michaud, who was standing about 300 feet west of the object along the same street. The hovering object was "dark" in color and had a "torpedo-shaped body." It was stationary in the air, hovering about 50 feet above the tops of the nearest buildings.

L-R: *Vermont Governor Urban A. Woodbury and Roman Catholic Bishop John S. Michaud*

From where he was standing, Michaud said the object appeared to be about six feet long and about eight inches in diameter. It seemed to be crackling with electricity, or some form of energy, said Michaud, "with here and there tongues of fire issuing from spots on the surface resembling red-hot unburnished copper." Michaud added that the object was "surrounded by a halo of dim light, some 20 feet in diameter."

The strange object was also seen by a man named Alvaro Adsit, who was standing in front of his place of business at the corner of College and Mechanic streets. A third witness, described only as a "young man who was looking out of a window in The Strong theater building." Yet another witness stated that he thought the object had struck the center of College Street and then bounced back up into the sky; however, no damage to the street was found.

Although the object was stationary when Michaud first observed it, he noticed that it suddenly began to move "rather slowly" to the south, going out of view beyond "Dolan Brothers' store." As the object moved, its outer covering, or hull, "seemed rupturing in places and through these the intensely red flames issued."

> **SAW BALL OF FIRE.**
>
> **Electrical Disturbance That Startled Burlingtonians Yesterday Noon.**
>
> A forerunner to one of the series of heavy and frequent thunderstorms that have characterized the early summer in this vicinity startled Burlingtonians yesterday just before noon. Without any preliminary disturbance of the atmosphere, there was a sharp report, the like of which is seldom heard. It was much louder in the business section of the city than elsewhere, and particularly in the vicinity of Church and College streets. People rushed to the street or to windows to learn what had happened and when a horse was seen flat in the street in front of the Standard Coal & Ice company's office it was the general impression that the animal had been struck by lightning and killed. This theory was not long entertained, however, as the horse was soon struggling to regain his feet, which he soon did with the asistance of many men who disconnected the harness from the wagon, and was found to be all right.
>
> Ex-Governor Woodbury and Bishop Michaud were standing on the corner of Church and College streets in conversation when the report startled them. In talking with a Free Press man later in the day Governor Woodbury said his first thought was that an explosion had occurred somewhere in the immediate vicinity and he turned, expecting to see bricks flying through the air. Bishop Michaud was facing the east and saw a ball of fire rushing through the air, apparently just east of the National Biscuit company's building. Alvaro Adsit, who was standing in front of his place of business at the corner of College and Mechanic street, also saw the ball of fire, as did a young man who was looking out of a window in The Strong theatre building. Another man with a vivid imagination declared that the ball struck the center of College street near the Standard Coal & Ice company's office, knocked the horse down by the jar and then bounded up again to some undefined point in the sky. He was unable to find any dent in the pavement, however, and in the absence of any explanation from the horse as to his actions, it is supposed the animal was frightened by the noise, jumped and slipped, having been hitched rather short. The unusual disturbance was followed in a few minutes by a downpour of rain which continued, with a brief interruption, for nearly two hours.

The Burlington (Vermont) Free Press, Jul. 3, 1907, p. 7

There ensued an explosion. Michaud said, "My first impression was that it was some explosive shot from the upper portion of the Hall furniture store... There was no odor, that I am aware of, perceptible

EARLY 20th CENTURY UFOs

after the disappearance of the phenomenon, nor was there any damage done, so far as known to me."

Former Vermont governor Urban Woodbury said his first thought was that an explosion had occurred somewhere in the immediate vicinity and he turned, expecting to see bricks flying through the air.

According to newspaper accounts, the only known damage or casualty was a horse that had been standing in the street in front of the Standard Coal & Ice company office but was knocked down flat onto the street. The newspaper said, "It was the general impression that that animal had been struck by lightning and killed." However, moments later, the horse regained its feet with the assistance of several men, who disconnected its harness from a wagon to which it was hitched.

Obviously a skilled and careful observer, Michaud noted the atmospheric conditions at the time of the sighting: "Although the sky was entirely clear overhead, there was an angry looking cumulonimbus cloud approaching from the northwest; otherwise, there was absolutely nothing to lead us to expect anything so remarkable. And strange to say, although the downpour of rain following this phenomenon, perhaps twenty minutes later, lasted at least half an hour, there was no indication of any other flash of lighting or sound of thunder."

Michaud was deeply impressed by what he saw and continued trying to analyze it in his mind for a long time afterward. He later wrote, "Four weeks

AMERICAN SIGHTINGS: 1900-1919

have passed since the occurrence of this event, but the picture of that scene and the terrific concussion caused by it are vividly before me, while the crashing sound still rings in my ears. I hope I may never hear or see a similar phenomenon, at least at such close range."

> **MADE VIVID IMPRESSION.**
>
> **Bishop Michaud's Description of a Recent Celestial Phenomenon.**
>
> The following account of a remarkable phenomenon witnessed by the Rt. Rev. J. S. Michaud and heard by many at the time will be read with interest:
>
> Burlington, Vt., July 28, 1907.
> Mr. W. H. Alexander, Director, Local Office, U. S. Weather Bureau:
>
> Dear Sir:—In reply to your request of a recent date, asking me to give in my own words a description of the phenomenon seen by me on July 2, 1907, at about 11 a. m., I submit the following brief statement of facts concerning the event, as I remember them:
>
> I was standing on the corner of Church and College streets, just in front of the Howard bank, and facing east, engaged in conversation with ex-Governor Woodbury and A. A. Buell, when, without the slightest indication or warning, we were startled by what sounded like a most unusual and terrific explosion very near by. Raising my eyes and looking eastward along College street, I observed a torpedo-shaped body some 300 feet away, stationary in appearance and suspended in the air about 50 feet above the tops of the buildings. In size, it was about six feet long by eight inches in diameter, the shell or cover having a dark appearance, with here and there tongues of fire issuing from spots on the surface resembling red-hot unburnished copper. Although stationary when first noticed this object soon began to move, rather slowly, and disappeared over Dolan Brothers' store, southward. As it moved, the covering seemed rupturing in places and through these the intensely red flames issued. My first impression was that it was some explosive shot from the upper portion of the Hall furniture store. When first seen it was surrounded by a halo of dim light, some 20 feet in diameter. There was no odor, that I am aware of, perceptible after the disappearance of the phenomenon, nor was there any damage done, so far as known to me. Although the sky was entirely clear overhead, there was an angry looking cumulo-nimbus cloud approaching from the northwest; otherwise, there was absolutely nothing to lead us to expect anything so remarkable. And strange to say, although the downpour of rain following this phenomenon, perhaps twenty minutes later, lasted at least half an hour, there was no indication of any other flash of lightning or sound of thunder.
>
> Four weeks have passed since the occurrence of this event, but the picture of this scene and the terrific concussion caused by it are vividly before me, while the crashing sound still rings in my ears. I hope I may never hear or see a similar phenomenon, at least at such close range.
>
> Yours very truly,
> JOHN S. MICHAUD,
> Bp. of Burlington.

The Burlington (Vermont) Free Press, Aug. 3, 1907, p. 8

In this UFO case, the object described by eyewitness Michaud was very small as far as saucers go, and perhaps it was a remote-controlled drone or other type of pilotless craft. In this series of books, we have examined other UFO cases where witnesses described small aerial objects fitting the description of modern-day drone aircraft.

EARLY 20th CENTURY UFOs

Interestingly, in this case, the object disappeared from view following the sound of an "explosion," after which no damage or debris was found. This would indicate that the explosive sound might have come from the craft's propulsion system, as it accelerated away from the town.

Also noteworthy is the strange electrical activity seen on the hull of the ship by Michaud. The object seemed to exude energy, being surround by a halo of light that extended for 20 feet all around it and possessed strange electrical energy "with here and there tongues of fire issuing from spots on the surface resembling red-hot unburnished copper." Given the odd nature of the incident, the multiple witnesses, and the highly reliable eyewitnesses, this case is one of the most interesting UFO encounters of the early 20th century.

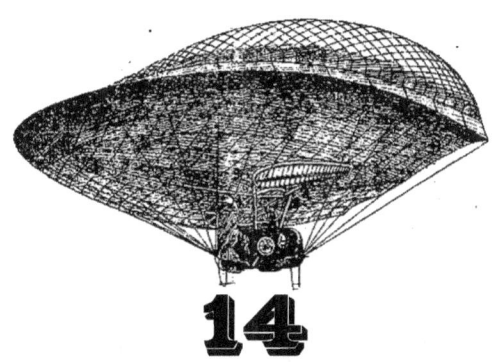

14
ALL HALLOWS EVE AIRSHIP
October 31, 1908
Bridgewater, Massachusetts

DURING THE EARLY morning hours of Halloween 1908, residents of Bridgewater, Massachusetts, located about 30 miles south of Boston, received an early "trick or treat" visit from a strange aerial object equipped with a super powerful spotlight. The incident followed a number of other reports of an airship with a bright light from throughout New England.

The story began shortly before 4 a.m. as two undertakers, Philip Prophett and John Flynn, were driving down Bridgewater's main street. They noticed in the sky above them "a bright light" that "resembled a searchlight."

EARLY 20th CENTURY UFOs

*Airship with Searchlight
(Courtesy Steve Baxter / Flickr)*

The powerful beam was traveling "at a rapid rate" while also moving closer to the Earth. An article appearing in the *Boston (Massachusetts) Globe* on the same day as the sighting, said, "The light was then played upon the earth beneath, as though operated by someone who wished to learn where he was. Then the light ascended, Prophett and Flynn say, until it reached a high elevation, when it disappeared in the direction of Plymouth."

According to the newspaper account, the object moved eastward, toward the coastal community of Plymouth, located 20 miles away from Bridgewater.

Significantly, the *Boston Globe* reported that the object was not any known airship. "All of the balloons in which ascensions are made in this state are accounted for today. The *Pittsfield in the Heart of the Berkshires* is a Pittsfield awaiting shipment to Fitchburg; the *North Adams No. 1* is at North Adams, where an ascension is to be made today; the *Greylock* was used yesterday in an ascension by William Van Sleet, and landed near Whately, and the balloon *Boston* is in New York being repaired." The newspaper added, "Stories of a mysterious bright light, believed by those who have seen it to have come from a balloon have been heard all over New England. Last summer several such reports came from the vicinity of Bristol, Conn., and later the same phenomenon was observed near Pittsfield. Persons at White River Junction, Vt., have also told of seeing a similar light, and last week persons at Ware reported that an illuminated balloon had passed over the town during the early hours of the morning. In all these cases, however, no balloon could be found, all the known air ships being accounted for at the time."

Bridewater, Mass., Circa 1850

EARLY 20th CENTURY UFOs

Searchlight Used by Russian Troops in 1904

In analyzing this close encounter, it is important to note that in 1908, there were few light sources capable of producing the intensely bright light described by witnesses Prophett and Flynn. The crude searchlights of the time were not portable, and battery technology was in its infancy. The chances seem slim that an unknown airship pilot decided to go aloft in the middle of the night carrying large numbers of batteries to power a huge searchlight that had been jury-rigged onto his airship. For what purpose would such a stunt be perpetrated?

AMERICAN SIGHTINGS: 1900-1919

ONLY SEEN IN BRIDGEWATER

Search of State for Balloon Futile.

Two Men Reported That Bright Light Was Played on Earth.

Then Ascended, to Pass Towards Plymouth.

A careful search by the Associated Press, covering practically every bit of territory between Bridgewater and the seacoast failed today to reveal any trace of a balloon, which was reported as passing over Bridgewater at an early hour this morning. The search failed to reveal that the balloon had been seen anywhere except in Bridgewater, and there only by two men who were driving down the main street from West Bridgewater to Bridgewater.

According to the Bridgewater reports, Philip Prophett and John Flynn, undertakers of that town, while driving into the town shortly before 4 o'clock, noticed a bright light in the sky above them. The light was not like that of a lantern, according to their reports, but resembled a searchlight. This light was traveling at a rapid rate, when suddenly it neared the earth.

The light was then played upon the earth beneath, as though operated by someone who wished to learn where he was. Then the light ascended, Prophett and Flynn say, until it reached a high elevation, when it disappeared in the direction of Plymouth.

All of the balloons in which ascensions are made in this state were accounted for today. The "Pittsfield in the Heart of the Berkshires" is at Pittsfield awaiting shipment to Fitchburg, the North Adams No. 1 is at North Adams, where an ascension is to be made today, the Greylock was used yesterday in an ascension by William Van Sleet, and landed near Whately, and the balloon Boston is in New York being repaired.

Stories of a mysterious bright light, believed by those who have seen it to have come from a balloon have been heard all over New England. Last summer several such reports came from the vicinity of Bristol, Conn, and later the same phenomenon was observed near Pittsfield.

Persons at White River Junction, Vt, have also told of seeing a similar light, and last week persons at Ware reported that an illuminated balloon had passed over the town during the early hours of the morning. In all these cases, however, no balloon could be found, all the known air ships being accounted for at the time.

Report That Started Search.

BRIDGEWATER, Oct 31—An unknown balloon passed over this town early today. The balloon carried a lantern, and when over the town the pilot brought it near the earth, apparently to get his bearings, then rose high in the air and disappeared in the direction of Plymouth.

The Boston (Massachusetts) Globe,
Oct. 31, 1908, p. 12

In an article about the incident in the *New York Sun* newspaper on November 1, 1908, the reporter pointed out, "Aeronauts are wondering if a mysterious airship, capable of navigating the skies no matter what the conditions are, is in existence and making nightly trips over New England."

As noted in the article, the manmade airships of 1908 could not easily accomplish the maneuvers that were observed by witnesses such as Prophett and Flynn in Bridgewater. So if it wasn't manmade, then who made it and what was its purpose? This question, unfortunately, remains unanswered even today.

EARLY 20th CENTURY UFOs

BIRDLIKE.

MYSTIFIES VALLEY.

Airship Flies Over Salton Sea.

Strange Craft Watched by a Number of Responsible People.

Disappears in the San Jacinto Mountains After Long Maneuvers.

Details of Machine Studied Through Glasses; Operator Hidden.

15
AIRSHIP OF THE SALTON SEA

June 1, 1909
Imperial Valley, California

BEGINNING ON THE EVENING of June 1, 1909 in the southern California towns of Imperial and Brawley, local residents reported seeing a huge, mysterious "aeroplane" hovering in the area of the Salton Sea, located to the north of both towns. The June 4 edition of the *Los Angeles Times* said, "All Imperial Valley is excited over reports of a mysterious airship which is taking nightly flights over Salton Sea. The monster ship has been seen by many persons in various localities, and the stories agree in general details."

EARLY 20th CENTURY UFOs

AEROPLANE IS SEEN BY RESIDENTS OF IMPERIAL

IMPERIAL, Cal., June 2.—A number of persons declare they saw an aeroplane at 6 o'clock last night come from the direction of the San Jacinto mountains and circle to the northward. They say it was so close they could distinguish the propeller. It has been said for several months that experiments on an aeroplane are in progress in the mountains.

Los Angeles (CA) Evening Express, June 2, 1909, p.14

The airship sighting was a significant enough story that on June 4, the *Los Angeles Times* devoted about a fourth of its front page to it. The story was also carried in many other state newspapers and several papers outside California. The *Los Angeles Times* related the stories of several eyewitnesses: "... a short time after sunset. W. D. Conser, a merchant of Imperial, and his wife were among the first to observe the moving object in the sky. They were driving into Imperial from the country and stopped their team to observe the strange sight. At first it appeared to be stationary at a point directly over Salton Sea near the intake of the Alamo and New rivers. Then the airship began a rapid flight, swerving from a southern course to one directly northwest and apparently passing directly across Salton Sea at its widest point until it disappeared in the shadows of the San Jacinto Mountains."

AMERICAN SIGHTINGS: 1900-1919

Edge of the Salton Sea Near Superstition Mountain (University of Southern California Libraries and the California Historical Society)

The *Times* also related the observation of a group of twenty men in Brawley: "Securing a field glass they closely studied the machine. Its appearance was that of a basket fastened between two wide wings, and when the turn was made it is said the propeller could be plainly seen, while the railings of the basket stood forth clearly against the sky, but the observers were unable to distinguish any persons in the basket. The huge machine was handled apparently without difficulty and the turn was made smoothly and at good speed."

One day later, on June 2, the strange airship was once again seen, appearing at about the same time and in the same vicinity as the evening before.

The article in the *Times* pointed out that if an airship inventor wanted to find an isolated spot in

EARLY 20th CENTURY UFOs

which to carry out secret experiments, they could not find a more suitable spot than the San Jacinto Mountains. "The western slope of the San Jacinto Mountains is one of the most precipitous to be found in California and for a machine using the sliding principal the site would offer a fine opportunity for experiments, while its isolated position would protect the experimenters from intrusion until such time as they were ready to make public of their inventions."

The report continued, "Rumors have been current for several months that men had gone into the San Jacinto Mountains from some Coachella Valley point to conduct experiments with a flying machine, but their movements were kept from the public. It is believed that the appearances of the past two nights are results of their successful invention."

The problem with these reports of mysterious inventors is that no such persons were ever identified. History tells us that no inventors or inventions were ever revealed to have been tested at the Salton Sea in 1909.

An article in the *San Francisco Chronicle* on June 5 sought to explain the airship sightings as an "atmospheric freak." Claiming that people were actually seeing objects on the ground, such as trees and houses, reflected in the sky above them, the newspaper said, "The mirage was conspicuous this evening for a few minutes and was viewed with wonderment by man people...." However, this explanation was not universally accepted.

AMERICAN SIGHTINGS: 1900-1919

It seems particularly interesting that eyewitnesses saw what they described, in clear detail, as a flying apparatus of some sort. They did not say they saw trees and houses. Was this simply a case of a celestial Rorschach test, where the witnesses were interpreting what they saw in the sky based on what was popular in their era? In any event, the mystery surrounding the Salton Sea airship sightings remains...

EARLY 20th CENTURY UFOs

MYSTERY AIRSHIP FLOATS BY

Norfolk Hears Of Man And Woman Who Appeared In Sky.

Norfolk, Va., May 1.—The spectacle of a mysterious airship, occupied by a man and a woman, passing over Hampton Roads, in the vicinity of Sewell's Point, was witnessed by more than 50 persons in that vicinity yesterday, according to apparently well-authenticated reports brought to Norfolk.

Those who saw the strange air craft stated that it resembled an automobile without wheels and that it was moved by a long propeller. The aeroplane did not descend in this section.

The Baltimore (Maryland) Sun, May 2, 1909, p. 5

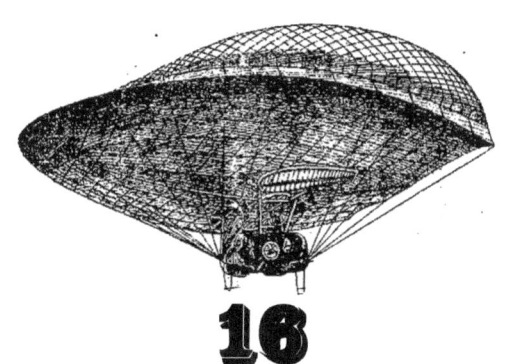

16
INVASION OF THE PIGEON PEOPLE
Spring 1910
Violetville, Maryland

IN 1979, RESPECTED UFO researcher Ted Bloecher released the publication "The Humanoid Catalog," compiled with David Webb and Lex Mebane, which included an amazing close encounter of the third kind that happened in Violetville, Maryland [a suburb of Baltimore], in the summer of 1910 [date uncertain], when the eyewitness was a very young boy.

In April 1969, a telephone call came in to the UFO group known as the National Investigations Committee on Aerial Phenomena (NICAP). The caller was a resident of Westminster, Maryland,

EARLY 20th CENTURY UFOs

who gave his name as Lawrence Joseph Crone, age 63.

Crone wanted to report a UFO encounter that he experienced as a boy. To the best of his recollection, the incident occurred around the year 1910, and it happened in Violetville, Maryland, where his family lived at the time.

Crone told his story separately to both Bloecher and to fellow NICAP investigator Thomas P. Deuley. Both men dutifully took the data down and later compared notes on what Crone told them.

The witness stated that in the summer of the year in question, he was standing in a baseball field near his home when he noticed a metallic blimp-shaped or cigar-shaped aerial craft descending from the sky.

Crone described the object as being brown in color and approximately 100 feet in length or "twice the length of a railroad car." The craft had a series of rectangular windows that appeared to be made of glass tinted in varying colors.

The strange craft hovered with an "oscillating" motion over a pine tree located 200 feet away from the baseball field where Crone stood.

As Crone viewed the hovering airship, he focused on one of the transparent windows and noticed that humanoid figures were visible inside the vessel. The humanoids were looking out of their ship, although Crone was not certain whether they were looking at him.

Although humanoid in appearance, the creatures were clearly not human. Their heads and necks were "like pigeons," indicating large round eyes, and a thick neck.

Pigeon (Courtesy info9srinivas/Pixabay)

However, their heads were pointed, or they wore pointed headwear - Crone could not be sure which. They had no nose and no ears. Their faces were flat and chinless, and Crone described their eyes as "two round spots or holes." As far as the mouth, it was merely a slit.

Some of the creatures' features were obviously hard for him to distinguish due to his distance (200 feet) from the craft. He thought the beings were covered with a soft-looking gray gown or fur - or perhaps they were wearing a light-colored gown. He was not sure if this was their natural body covering or whether it was a garment of some kind. As he watched the activity at the window of the ship, he noticed that the entities seemed to take turns coming to the window to look out. Groups of two or three of the creatures would stand and look

EARLY 20th CENTURY UFOs

out the window, before yielding their spot to others of their kind.

To the best of his recollection, Crone thinks he saw a total of twenty of the humanoids inside the ship.

Until this point, Crone was transfixed by what he was viewing, but he finally had the idea to find others around him to witness what he was seeing. He called out to two young men, calling their attention to the strange object, but as soon as they saw the ship, they began screaming and running away.

At a later point, Crone's mother arrived at the scene and was able to view the UFO, which then slowly moved upward and departed the area.

As a footnote to this remarkable story, Bloecher notes that Crone "has had at least 12 UFO sightings during his lifetime."

Unfortunately, no further information was gathered, and Lawrence Crone passed away on June 15, 1984, at the age of 78.

```
10-   1910 (± 2 yrs), Summer   Morning   Vidotville, Maryland              Type A

      Lawrence J. Crone, then aged 4-7, saw a blimp-like ship hovering lower
  than a tree 200 ft away, with an oscillating motion. It was about twice the
  length of a railroad car, and had windows of different colors of glass. Through
  the clear glass he could see entities watching him. They had heads & necks
  "like pigeons", with pointed heads, no nose or ears, and "2 spots for eyes."
  Their faces were flat, with no chin, and covered with a soft-looking gray down,
  like fur. He called the ship to the attention of 2 young men, who screamed and
  ran away. His mother came out and also saw the UFO, which moved away slowly.
      The witness has had at least 12 UFO sightings during his lifetime.

  Investigator: none.

  Source: Witness's phone call to NICAP, April 1969.
```

Report of Bloecher's Initial Phone Conversation with Crone (NICAP)

Looking at historical data on "mystery airship" sighting around the same period, the authors found

AMERICAN SIGHTINGS: 1900-1919

a significant sighting in on May 1, 1909, in nearby Norfolk, Virginia, located about 200 miles south of Violetville. More than fifty witnesses saw the strange object, which "resembled an automobile without wheels ... moved by a long propeller," according to an account in the *Baltimore (Maryland) Sun* newspaper. More interestingly, two humanoids were seen aboard the ship, reported to be a male and a female.

The Baltimore (Md.) Sun, Dec. 23, 1909, p. 1

In December 1909, Baltimore residents were captivated by the story of a high-flying mystery airship seen several hundred miles away, in Worcester, Massachusetts on December 22, 1909. Thousands of eyewitnesses watched as the object shone down "a searchlight of tremendous power," as it circled the city several times, flying at an altitude of about 2,000 feet. Although it was hard to see the actual ship because of the bright light, the

EARLY 20th CENTURY UFOs

newspaper account of the incident said, "The dark mass of the ship could be dimly seen behind the light."

Also reported in the *Baltimore Sun* was a mysterious airship that was seen down in Tennessee and Alabama on January 12, 1910. The fast-moving ship was travelling at a high altitude and observers on the ground could hear "the chugging of the engine."

STRANGE AIRSHIP SEEN

Reported As Travelling High And Fast From Two Places In South.

Chattanooga, Tenn., Jan. 12. — At 9 o'clock this morning an airship passed over Chattanooga at a great altitude. Thousands saw the craft and the chugging of the engine could be heard.

Tonight a dispatch from Huntsville, Ala., announces that the airship passed over that city, traveling at a fast rate of speed.

The Baltimore (Maryland) Sun, Jan. 13, 1910, p. 1

The unidentified vessel was seen over Chattanooga, Tennessee, at 9 a.m. and was then seen in the evening at Huntsville, Alabama, 102 miles to the west-southwest of Chattanooga.

Of course, it is uncertain if any of these other airship sightings were related in any way to the amazing 1910 encounter experienced by Lawrence

AMERICAN SIGHTINGS: 1900-1919

Crone in Violetsville, Maryland. However, they do establish that the area around Maryland was experiencing airship activity during the same time period (1909 - 1910).

As for how to explain what Crone claims he saw, that is probably well beyond the realm of possibility, given the limited data available about the case.

EARLY 20th CENTURY UFOs

Dr. J. Allen Hynek

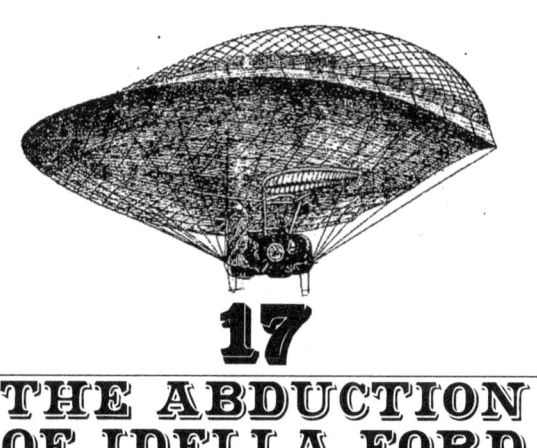

17
THE ABDUCTION OF IDELLA FORD
May 1911
Piqua, Ohio

THOUGH ALIEN abductions have possibly been occurring since the dawn of time, the idea of alien abduction didn't truly seep into the public consciousness until the Betty and Barney Hill case of 1961. This was the first instance to include the major characteristics of what we now consider a typical abduction, including missing time, strange creatures, and bodily evidence that the witnesses had been through some sort of physical exam.

While driving in New Hampshire's White Mountains on the night of September 19, 1961, the Hills saw a bright light in the sky that seemed to be

EARLY 20th CENTURY UFOs

pursuing them. It turned out to be an oddly shaped, 40-foot-long UFO with flashing, multicolored lights. Both Betty and Barney Hill "blacked out" and experienced "missing time." It was only later, while under hypnosis, that they both described being taken aboard the UFO, where a series of apparent medical examinations were conducted on them by a group of strange humanoid creatures. The two abductees were haunted by their experience, suffering from nightmares and other problems for many years after their encounter.

Betty & Barney Hill (Courtesy Kathleen Marden)

In recent years, researchers have begun to see a correlation between abductees and post-traumatic stress disorder. Some abductees find the memories of their abductions so disturbing that they sometimes develop psychological problems. Some

AMERICAN SIGHTINGS: 1900-1919

will even commit suicide for fear of being abducted again.

In late November of 1973, world-famous astronomer and UFO researcher J. Allen Hynek received a letter from a 77-year-old named Elsie Fox Shirley who described the traumatic experience of an abductee that predated the Betty and Barney Hill case by exactly 50 years.

The incident happened to Shirley's sister, Idella Fox Ford (1876-1913), in 1911. At the time, Idella was a 36-year-old music teacher and mother of two sons – Bernard, 12, and Floyd, 10. She lived just outside of Piqua, Ohio, in Union County. She was divorced from Dr. Carl Ford, of Broadway, Ohio, a physician and preacher, whom she married in 1898.

In mid-May 1911, Idella boarded a train to go visit her grandmother, who lived 40 miles away in Broadway. Conveniently, her grandmother actually lived across the street from the railroad depot, so Idella could simply walk there when she arrived.

In a shocking turn of events, after arriving in Broadway, Idella stumbled into her grandmother's home in a state of extreme emotional and physical duress. Although many years would pass before she finally revealed what happened to her, she eventually told family members that "they" had come from sky to take her, and she lived the rest of her life in fear of these mysterious beings that might some day come back and "take" not only her, but other members of her family. More specifically, she was terribly frightened that the beings would "destroy" her and her family.

EARLY 20th CENTURY UFOs

In addition to the bizarre account of beings from the sky, Idella also had strange marks on her body that apparently resulted from her "abduction," if that is what it was. First, something very hot had seared her face, and her tongue was strangely swollen. On her calves were three indentations that seemed to have been made by a hand with only three fingers. Interestingly, grey aliens are often depicted with only three fingers and one thumb on each hand.

This was the secret that finally came out after many years of strange silence. Right after the incident happened, Idella was so distraught that her grandmother called Idella's mother, Mrs. Ida Fox, to come at once. Ida, and her son, raced to Broadway from Delaware, Ohio, 14 miles away, as quickly as they could by horse and buggy.

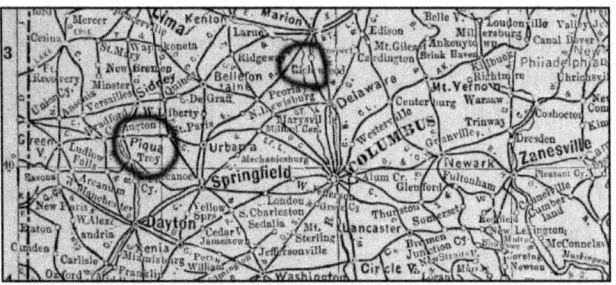

1911 Ohio Map with the Key Areas of this Incident Circled, Piqua on the left and Broadway on the right.

At the same time, one of Idella's other brothers travelled to Idella's home to look in on her two boys. He asked them if their mother had seemed upset when she left, but they said she seemed fine and happy when she boarded the train. What exactly happened to Idella during her voyage was a great mystery for many years, with Idella offering few clues and only rarely providing minor hints about her ordeal.

Many people tried to get Idella to talk about the experience. When asked, Idella would become so upset as to become incoherent. Several doctors examined her, one of which was her brother, D.C. Fox, and all agreed that something unusual had happened to her. The physical manifestations of her ordeal were clearly present on her body, and her overall behavior had changed dramatically since the incident.

Mrs. Idella Ford Attempts Suicide.

Word was received at Broadway, Tuesday, that Mrs. Idella Ford, a former resident of that village, had attempted suicide by throwing herself in the Scioto river, near Radnor, Delaware county. She was rescued in time to save her life.

Mrs. Ford is a daughter of Mrs. Ida L. Fox, who lives on the old Cohen place, near Radnor. The daughter has been living in Piqua for several years, where she conducted a boarding house. She came to the home of her mother on a visit the first of the week, and her mind is thought to be unbalanced by domestic troubles which have extended over a period of several years.

Marysville (OH) Journal-Tribune, Nov. 26, 1912, p. 3

EARLY 20th CENTURY UFOs

When she finally disclosed her story, she did so only to her mother and her sister Elsie, who years later sent a letter to J. Allen Hynek about her sister's abduction.

Sadly, Idella's life did not have a happy ending. After the ordeal, she and her sons moved in with her mother, and Idella lapsed into a suicidal frame of mind. On one occasion, the family stopped her from jumping off a high beam located in a barn. Another time, she was rescued from trying to drown herself in the nearby Scioto river.

With the concept of alien visitation and abduction being totally unknown in 1911, Idella's mother concluded that her daughter was insane and had her committed to the Columbus State Mental Hospital in Columbus, Ohio. After committing Idella, Mrs. Fox burned Idella's journal, in which she gave details about her bizarre encounter. Mrs. Fox felt that the journal entries were simply the ramblings of a mentally disturbed person and destroyed them all.

On October 13, 1913, after being at the state hospital for exactly 10 months, Idella hanged herself in her hospital room. As reported in the local newspapers she tore pieces from her bedsheet and fastened the cloth to the top horizontal metal bar covering her window. A report in the *Richwood (Ohio) Gazette* said, "Standing for several hours with her face pressed against one of the windows of the Columbus State hospital, Mrs. Idella Ford, a suicide, was seen by many patients and attendants Monday. Not knowing, however, that the woman was dead, no particular attention was paid to the fact that she stood in the window apparently looking out. About four o'clock Monday afternoon, considering the action of the patient to be unusual, an investigation was made, and the attendants were greatly shocked at finding a corpse in the window."

The article continued, "It is presumed that Mrs. Ford hanged herself quite early in the morning. She had tied a sheet about her neck, fastening one end to the iron bar at the top of the window in her room. When found, the tips of her toes were resting on the window sill."

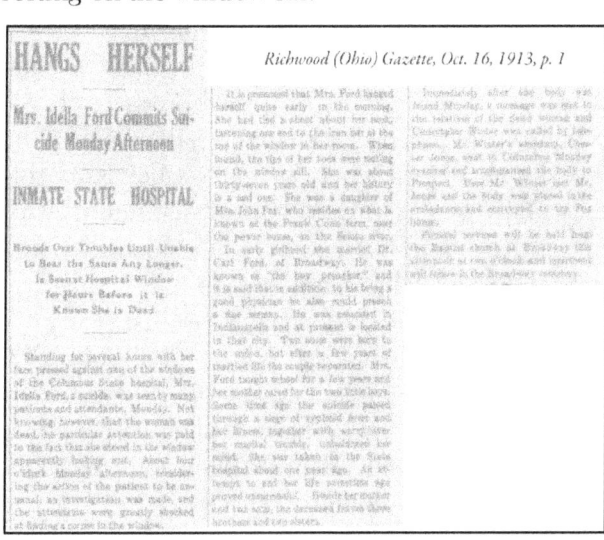

Richwood (Ohio) Gazette, Oct. 16, 1913, p. 1

The *Gazette* added a statement suggesting that Idella had been driven to madness by a recent illness, along with the trauma of her divorce. "Some time ago, the suicide passed through a siege of typhoid fever, and her illness, together with worry over her marital trouble, unbalanced her mind." Although the article mentions a previous suicide attempt, it does not discuss the strange encounter that happened to Idella in 1911.

In fact, no mention is made of her strange encounter in any of the notices published about her death. Her "abduction" story was clearly considered to be just the ravings of a deranged person. Interestingly, the account of her death given in The *Marion (Ohio) Star* on October 15, 1913, gives an alternate possible cause for her mental problems. The *Star* said, "Brooding over religious matters brought about her mental derangement." What "religious matters" would these have been? Is it possible that people overheard her talking about beings that came from the sky and "took" her, as well as her fears that these "sky beings" would come back and destroy her and her family? To someone unfamiliar with the context of what happened to Idella, it might sound like religious, apocalyptic visions.

Decades later, when Elsie learned about UFOs and alien abductions, she finally pieced together in her mind what might have really happened to Idella - that she had somehow been abducted back in 1911, and consequently, she wrote her letter to Dr. Hynek in 1973. This very sad and tragic story seems far too realistic to be dismissed as a fabrication. Significantly, we have been able to use the historical records to verify all of the information about the persons involved and most of the events mentioned by Elsie in her letter to Hynek.

AMERICAN SIGHTINGS: 1900-1919

> **MRS. IDELLA FORD COMMITS SUICIDE**
>
> Hangs Herself in State Hospital in Columbus.
>
> Mrs. Idella Ford, thirty-seven years of age, of Radnor township, committed suicide by hanging herself from the bars at the window of her room in the state hospital for the insane at Columbus, Tuesday morning. The unfortunate used strips torn from a sheet on her bed. An attendant discovered the body.
>
> Mrs. Ford was committed to the asylum February 12. Brooding over religious matters brought about her mental derangement.
>
> *The Marion (Ohio) Star, Oct. 15, 1913, p. 4*

But truthfully, could Idella have been abducted from a moving train? There have certainly been stranger tales of abduction. Some abductees have reported being taken from moving automobiles and from rooms with locked doors and no windows. If not from a moving train, perhaps Idella was taken during one of the rest stops along the train route between her home and her destination.

EARLY 20th CENTURY UFOs

The disaster of the biggest steamer of the world "S. S. Titanic" sinking on an iceberg - April 15th, 1912

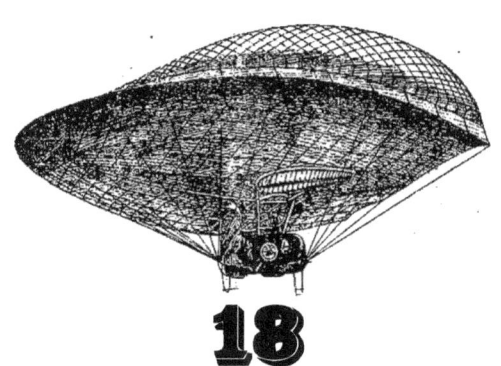

18
UFOs OVER THE TITANIC
April 15, 1912
North Atlantic Ocean

IT IS PERHAPS the world's best-known disaster story - the sinking of the *RMS Titanic* on April 15, 1912, after striking an iceberg in the North Atlantic while steaming to New York City. Of the estimated 2,224 passengers and crew aboard the doomed ship, more than 1,500 died in the freezing sea. For the survivors, watching the ship go down from lifeboats and floating pieces of debris was certainly the most horrible and traumatic experience of their lives. The eyewitness accounts of the tragedy certainly reflect that horror, but they also may reflect something else. Over the years, some researchers have suggested that the survivors of the *Titanic* disaster may have seen mysterious, brightly illuminated flying objects hovering over the scene of the sinking.

RMS Titanic (By F.G.O. Stuart [1843-1923] via Wikimedia Commons)

In examining the accounts given later by the survivors, interestingly a number of them commented on strange sights they saw in the night sky as they floated in the ocean, having just been saved from one of the worst tragedies in history. The most remarkable of these accounts was given by a young science teacher from England, Lawrence Beesley, who escaped the sinking of the ship in one of its few lifeboats. Beesley - an intelligent, educated observer of nature and events - gave stunning testimony of everything he saw from his lifeboat, including a strange display of

AMERICAN SIGHTINGS: 1900-1919

"stars" in the sky that seemed unusually near and bright. In fact, they seemed to be so near and so close to the horizon that the survivors "were often deceived into thinking they were lights of a ship."

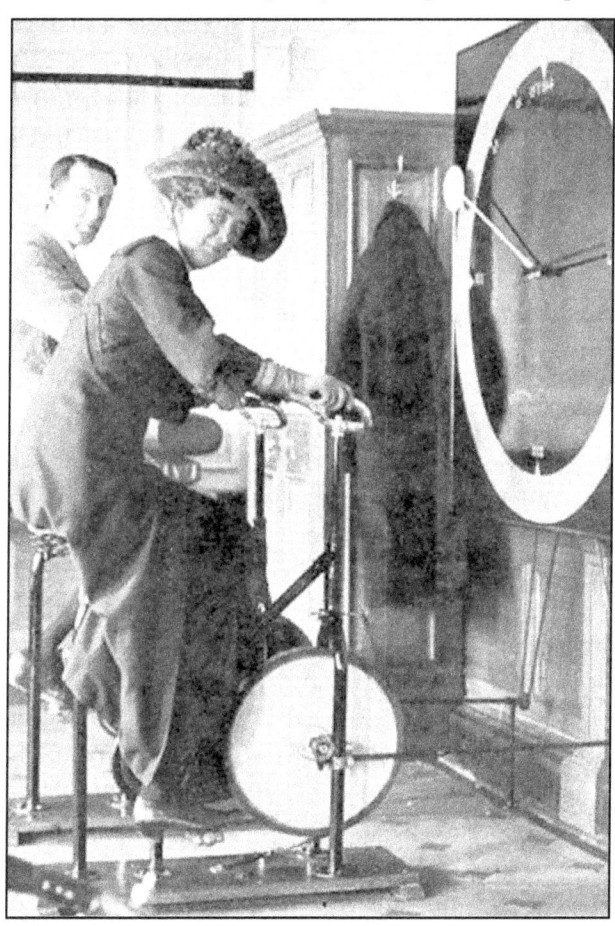

Lawrence Beesley (left) and an Unidentified Passenger in the Exercise Room of the Titanic (Central News & Illustrations Bureau)

EARLY 20th CENTURY UFOs

In *The Story of the Titanic As Told by its Survivors*, Beesley wrote, "... the climatic conditions were extraordinary. The night was one of the most beautiful I have ever seen; the sky without a single cloud to mar the perfect brilliance of the stars, clustered so thickly together...."

Upon continuing to examine the strange character of the stars, Beesley added that "each star seemed, in the keen atmosphere, free from any haze, to have increased its brilliance tenfold and to twinkle and glitter with a staccato flash...."

Some of the stars seemed so close in the sky to them that Beesley said, "They seemed so near, and their light so much more intense than ever before.... The stars seemed really to be alive and to talk." He goes on to mention that as the bright stars neared the horizon, he could see a bright reflection from them cast upon the water.

"In the evidence before the United States Senate Committee, the captain of one of the ships near us that night said the stars were so extraordinarily bright near the horizon that he was deceived into thinking that they were ships' lights."

Beesley concluded his description of this aerial phenomenon by saying, "Those who were afloat will all agree with that statement: we were often deceived into thinking they [stars low on the horizon] were lights of a ship."

Beesley's amazing account of incredibly bright stars near the horizon that seemed to "be alive and to talk" was mostly lost in all the horror and pain associated with the awful tragedy of the *Titanic* disaster. However, in analyzing what happened that night, with so many human souls crying out as they were dragged down to an icy death in the frigid North Atlantic, Beesley's account of these strange stars seems to cry out to us all these decades later.

Engraving by Willy Stöwer: Der Untergang der Titanic

Is it possible that the sinking of the *Titanic*, one of the most pivotal events in human history, was being observed by beings hovering in airships nearby? If so, were these beings from another planet or perhaps from another time period? Whoever they might have been, they obviously had a clear directive that prevented them from interfering in the events that were tragically unfolding before them. They were forced to watch helplessly as 1,500 human lives were snuffed out before their very eyes.

Perhaps they were students of science, like Lawrence Beesley, visiting the scene of the tragedy to study and understand all that transpired there. If

EARLY 20th CENTURY UFOs

they were beings from another intelligent civilization visiting our Earth to observe us, it stands to reason that they would want to view one of the most pivotal and historic events in all human history.

Prior to the sinking of the *Titanic*, another ship of the White Star Line had encountered something that remains unexplained to this very day. The White Star steamship *SS Naronic*, carrying 74 men, mysteriously disappeared along with all passengers and crew in February of 1893, while following the same Liverpool to New York route that the *Titanic* would later follow. The only evidence ever found of the *Naronic*'s existence were two empty lifeboats, one of which was found within 19 miles of where the Titanic later sank.

The March 6, 1893 edition of *The New York Evening World* said, "The fate of the big freight carrier Naronic is still a mystery, and as the days go by without any news from her, the believe that she has gone to the bottom gains more adherents in shipping circles." The same newspaper, several weeks later, reported that both the wife of *Naronic*'s captain and the wife of its First Officer had "gone insane through despair caused by the loss of their husbands and have been placed in an asylum."

Also noteworthy about the *Naronic*'s disappearance is that it drew much interest from the paranormal community of the time. A number of self-proclaimed spiritualists and mediums became involved in trying to determine the fate of the missing ship. A consensus developed among them that the ship had not sunk and would soon be discovered.

Sister Ship to the SS Naronic *was the* Bovic, *Shown Above*

Whereas the sinking of the *Titanic* created a floating ocean of debris that was seen for months afterward, the *Naronic* left no such traces. Except for the two lifeboats, nothing was ever found of it. Also, most experts of the time felt that the *Naronic* was unlikely to have struck an iceberg and therefore were unable to determine a probable cause for its disappearance.

About the *Naronic* and other similar cases, paranormal researcher Charles Fort, in his 1931 book *Lo!*, wrote, "It may be that something of which the inhabitants of this Earth know nothing, is concerned in these disappearances, or seizures ... It may be that constructions from somewhere else have appeared upon this Earth and have seized crews of this Earth's ships."

Could the disappearance of the White Star liner *Naronic* be related to UFOs, as Fort suggested? If so, why were UFOs specifically interested in the

EARLY 20th CENTURY UFOs

ships of the White Star Line that were traveling along this route from Liverpool to New York?

*Charles Fort, Paranormal Researcher
(Circa 1920)*

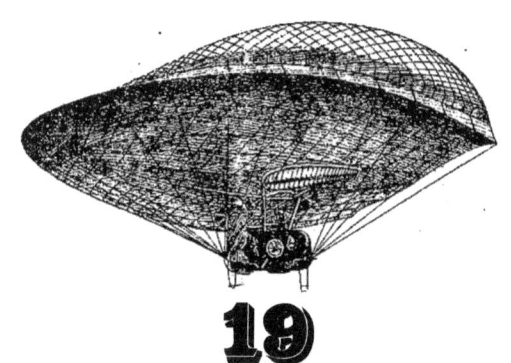

19

UFO CASTS SHADOW IN TEXAS

April 8, 1913
Fort Worth, Texas

IN *THE FLYING SAUCERS ARE REAL*, Donald E. Keyhoe's classic 1950 book, the author speaks of a strange celestial phenomenon that was observed over Fort Worth, Texas, on April 8, 1913. Keyhoe wrote, "A strange shadow was noted on the clouds at Fort Worth, Texas, on April 8, 1913. It appeared to be caused by some large body hovering motionless above the clouds. As the cloud layer moved, the shadow remained in the same position. Then it changed size, diminishing, and quickly disappeared, as if it had risen vertically. A report on this was given in the *Weather Bureau Review* of that year."

The unusual sighting began at about 6:30 p.m. The Weather Bureau stated, "The day had been generally cloudy and sultry, with occasional traces of precipitation... At 6:30 p.m., local time, a great bank of cumulonimbus presented itself in the western sky directly in the path of the sun. The top of this mass was of the usual 'Steam column' or thunderhead type, and to the southward dense streaks of falling rain were seen."

"As the sun sank lower behind the cloud, a shadow tip, surrounded by a faint penumbra, forced its way into the clear sky. At the moment of maximum intensity, the ghostly shadow reared fully 15 degrees above the parent cloud, a sight not to be forgotten. Surrounding the penumbra was a faint 'glory,' daintily and lightly colored."

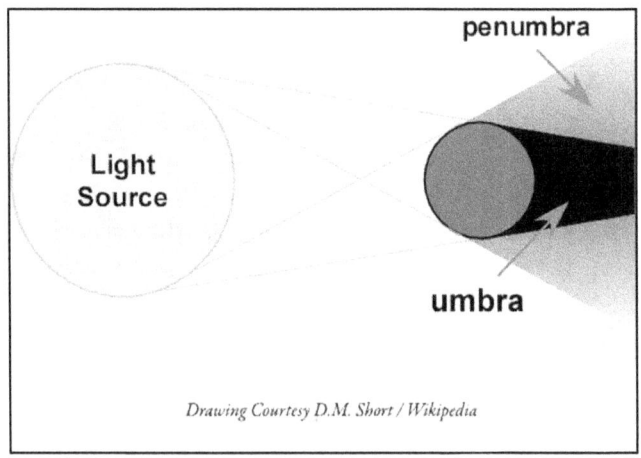

Drawing Courtesy D.M. Short / Wikipedia

CLOUD-SHADOW PROJECTION.

By Howard H. Martin, Assistant Observer, Fort Worth, Tex.

A peculiar and most interesting observation of the projection of cloud shadows was made at Fort Worth, Tex., on the evening of April 8, 1913. The phenomenon consisted essentially of a distinct and vivid shadow of an unseen prominence of cloud, projected over the main body of which it was a part, and screened upon a patch of clear sky at about 35° altitude.

The day had been generally cloudy and sultry, with occasional traces of precipitation. During the morning the higher clouds had moved steadily from the south and southwest, but the passage of a dry thunderstorm in the afternoon changed the direction to southeast. The lower clouds moved from the southeast during the morning hours, changing to southwest and west by night.

At 6.30 p. m., local time, a great bank of cumulo-nimbus presented itself in the western sky directly in the path of the sun. The top of this mass was of the usual "steam column" or thunderhead type, and to the southward dense streaks of falling rain were to be seen. To the eastward lay a greater bank of alto-stratus, and this, together with the western cloud, formed an admirable background for the phenomenon in the clear spot overhead.

As the sun sank lower behind the cloud a shadow tip, surrounded by a faint penumbra, forced its way into the clear sky. At the moment of maximum intensity the ghostly shadow reared fully 15° above the parent cloud, a sight not to be forgotten. Surrounding the penumbra was a faint "glory," daintily and lightly colored.

The duration of this phenomenon was comparatively short. By 6.45 p. m. the shadow had disappeared and the cloud bank greatly diminished in size, but the streaks of falling rain had become more intensified and were now accompanied by an occasional flash of zigzag lightning.

The sun set cloudy, sinking out of the cumulo-nimbus bank into a lower bank of alto-stratus. The phenomenon was followed within about two hours by a thunderstorm and copious precipitation. Although such phenomena are probably not rare, yet circumstances favorable to their observation are sufficiently so to render them worthy of note.

Monthly Weather Review, April 1913, p. 599

EARLY 20th CENTURY UFOs

The appearance of a penumbra confirms that a solid object had interposed itself between the sun's light and the observers on the ground. The umbra itself is, of course, the shadow.

Although the Weather Bureau insisted that the shadow upon the clouds was caused by the tip of a "cloud column" at a higher altitude casting its shadow on a bank of clouds that was below it, a number of researchers including Donald Keyhoe and Charles Fort seriously questioned the scientific explanation.

From the perspective of Keyhoe and Fort, a large UFO, possibly a mothership, moved between the sun and the clouds, causing the shadow to appear to the observers on the ground.

A key point was that "as the cloud layer moved, the shadow remained in the same position," as Keyhoe pointed out. If the shadow had been caused by clouds upon other clouds, as the cloud layer moved, the shadow would have also moved. Instead, obviously, there was an object hovering in a stationary position behind the clouds.

When the UFO did finally move, it did so by first diminishing in size, indicating that it was moving upward, rising vertically, until it was out of view. But obviously, a group of government-salaried scientists, especially in the early 20th century, would never admit the possibility that this event was something other than a perfectly natural weather phenomenon.

Over the years since 1913, UFOs have been observed drifting in and out of cloud formations, seemingly using the clouds as a means to remain

AMERICAN SIGHTINGS: 1900-1919

hidden from view. Some researchers have even conjectured that some UFOs are able to generate a cloud-like mist around themselves in order to stay out of sight. If the shadow seen over Fort Worth in 1913 was actually a UFO, what was it doing there? Was it merely engaged in observing the puny humans below?

Interesting questions, one and all.

Downtown Fort Worth (Lib. Of Congress)

EARLY 20th CENTURY UFOs

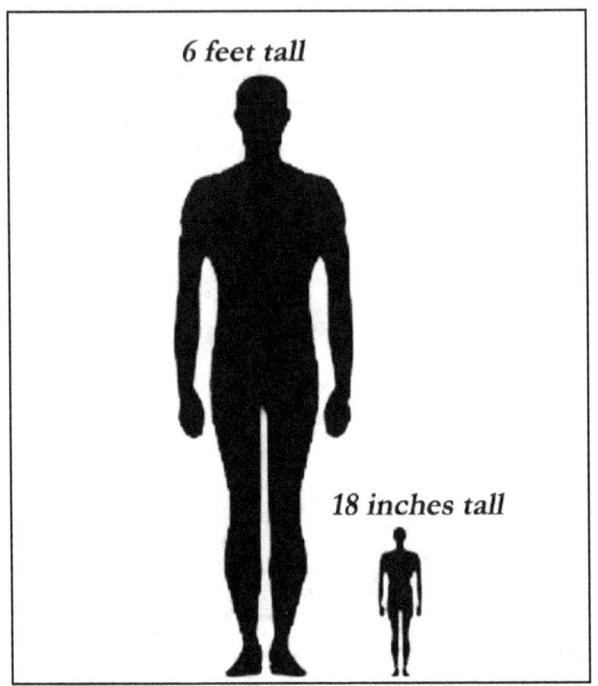

The Little Creature's Height Compared to a 6 Foot Man

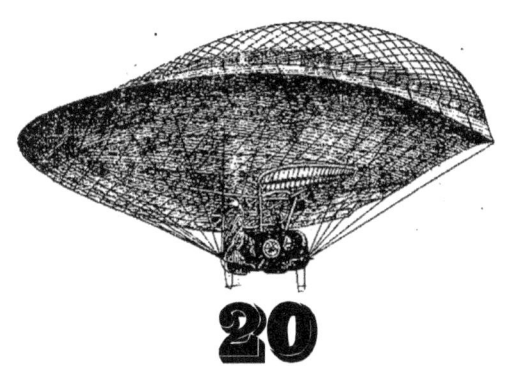

20
THE LITTLE GREEN MAN OF TEXAS
1913 or 1914
Farmersville, Texas

TEXAS WAS apparently the place for little humanoids falling out of the sky during the turn of the 19th century. While many people today are aware of the reported 1897 UFO crash of Aurora, Texas, where an alien was said to have met his demise, fewer are aware of another similar case in 1913.

In January of 1978 a man named Lawrence Jones wrote a letter to the J. Allen Hynek Center for UFO Studies in Chicago. Jones claimed that in the month of May in either the year 1913 or 1914, his grandfather, Silbie Latham, had witnessed the

EARLY 20th CENTURY UFOs

death of a strange humanoid creature. Jones wrote in his letter, "My grandfather has a most solid reputation for truth and honesty but has never told of this because of fear of ridicule ... He has agreed to tell this only after much prompting and encouragement from me, his history-oriented grandson. He would take a polygraph or be hypnotized or whatever you need. There is no question in my mind that he is telling the truth." [Source: *Fairies: Real Encounters with Little People* by Janet Bord].

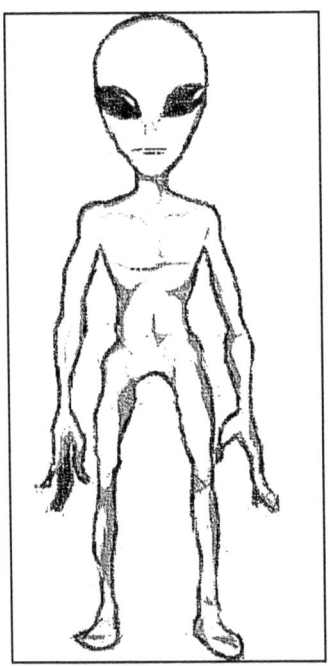

Another reason that Latham didn't come forward with his story would have been due to the times. Back in 1913, the idea of aliens, let alone

AMERICAN SIGHTINGS: 1900-1919

descriptions of them, had yet to seep into the public consciousness. But by the 1970s, when interest in the paranormal and UFOs reached new heights, the idea of an alien sighting didn't seem quite so strange anymore.

Upon reception of Jones's letter, the Center for UFO Studies (CUFOS) set up an interview between Silbie Latham, who was then 77 years old, and Larry Sessions of the Museum of Natural History of Fort Worth. The interview took place in April of 1978. During the meeting, Latham recalled his boyhood experience on a farm 2.5 miles away from Farmersville, Texas [the spot of an airship sighting in 1897, by the way].

Latham's encounter with the strange creature took place in either the year 1913 or 1914. He was out chopping cotton with his two brothers, Sid and Clyde, when they suddenly heard their dogs begin howling as if in distress. As the howling went on for some time, Clyde said, "Let's see what's going on with the dogs. They seem quite shaken."

Clyde arrived at the spot first, which was about 60 to 75 feet away on the other side of a picket fence. He was the first to see the strange sight, and as such called for his brothers to hurry and go look. "Boys, come look! It's a little man!" he shouted at the site where the dogs had cornered a small, humanoid figure, about eighteen inches tall.

Latham told Sessions that the creature looked like "he was sitting on something." Latham continued that, "He was looking toward the north. He was no more than 18 inches high and kind of a dark green color. He was the same smooth color all over. He didn't seem to have any shoes on, but I don't really remember his feet. His arms were hanging down just beside him, like they [grew] down the side of him. He had on a kind of hat that reminded me of a Mexican hat. It was a little round hat that looked like it was built onto him. He didn't have on any clothes."

This so-called hat is the strangest detail of all, and his comment that it was "built into him" implies this little green man wasn't wearing the hat, but it appeared to be a part of his anatomy – either that or the hat was part of a skin-tight suit. As it was, it seemed that Sessions couldn't tell if the dark green color of the body was the creature's actual skin or a skin-tight suit that somehow molded the "hat" to its head.

Latham continued, "Everything looked like a rubber suit including the hat. He just stood still. I guess he was just scared to death. Right after we got there, the dogs jumped him."

It was at that point that the dogs literally tore the little man apart. So much noise was made in the ruckus that the boys weren't able to tell if the poor creature made any noise or not, but they knew one thing: it had red blood. As the boys watched the gory spectacle, the dogs tore the thing's legs off which seeped red with blood. Even the internal organs looked like those belonging to a human being. Latham told Sessions, "Blood and guts went everywhere. The blood was red and the guts looked like guts look. We were all just country as hell and didn't know what to do... The dogs just chewed him to pieces."

AMERICAN SIGHTINGS: 1900-1919

With the creature torn apart and clearly dead, the boys didn't know what to do other than return to work while continuing to discuss the event. Latham said they would occasionally take a break to go look at the site of the killing throughout the day. Each time they did the dogs stuck closely to them and acted frightened or upset by the remains. The next day the remains were gone, presumably carried away by scavengers. Mysteriously, there wasn't even a trace of blood at the site.

When Sessions asked Latham why he and his brother didn't try to prevent the attack, Sessions answered, "We are just country guys and we did not know what to do with all this story. We must have been too much surprised." A slightly different quote from Latham is given in the book *Mysteries Around UFOs and Aliens* by Vikas Khatri: "We were all just scared as hell and didn't know what to do about it. I guess we were just too dumb."

The excuse seems valid and believable. The boys would no doubt be scared to approach the creature. Also, the sequence of events probably happened so quickly that they were too late to call the dogs off once the attack began. And, again, in 1913 the idea of aliens from outer space was a foreign concept. It is unlikely that the three teenage farm boys would have even entertained the notion that the humanoid should be saved in order that scientists could study it or its remains. According to author Albert S. Rosales, in his book *Humanoid Encounters: 1900-1929: The Others Amongst Us*, the boys did tell their parents, but their story was not believed.

Cover of Fate Magazine, Nov. 1978 (Courtesy FateMagCollector.com)

Sessions himself could not accept the truthfulness of the story, although he assessed that Latham was "a remarkable man." Although Sessions doubted that the event actually happened as described, he conceded, "There's no doubt [Latham] believes it happened, but that doesn't mean it did happen. Maybe he has an overactive imagination. Or maybe his brothers played a trick on him and he's sort of unconsciously embellished the story over the years." [*Alex Evans, "Encounters with Little Men," *FATE*, November 1978, pp. 83-85*]

It is important to note that Sessions was not a trained UFO investigator. He was asked to look into the case by CUFOs only because the organization had no trained investigators in the area; therefore, Sessions' skepticism about a UFO encounter is understandable. However, it is significant that Sessions was convinced that Latham truly believed the incident really happened. Latham passed away a year later, on October 21, 1979, at the age of 78, thereby ending any future attempts to interview him about his amazing experience.

And what of the Little Green Man? For starters, it was about half the size of a typical grey alien, which as their name implies are grey, not green. However, Latham wasn't the only person to ever spot a small humanoid of such diminutive stature. For instance, in 1804, Lewis and Clark heard tales of a small, isolated tribe of strange "little people" that stood 18 inches tall, possessed advanced weapon technology, and were shunned by all the neighboring Native American tribes. Then, in the 1830s, a fur trapper named Bob McCain claimed he rescued a two-foot-tall humanoid clad in green from an animal trap.

As if Latham's entity encounter were not odd enough, a couple of years later (in 1915 or 1916), Latham and one of his brothers had yet another strange incident. The boys saw a mysterious airship

EARLY 20ᵗʰ CENTURY UFOs

as they sat on their uncle's front porch in Celeste, Texas. They described the craft as being like "an airplane without wings" in that it was long and cylindrical. There was a bright light at the front and back of the craft.

Could their UFO sighting have been linked to their earlier encounter with the tiny humanoid? Perhaps Latham's experiences are proof that these sorts of odd paranormal events tend to occur to certain specific people, rather than just at random?!

21
HUNDREDS SEE FAST MOVING UFO
June 29, 1913
Lansing, Michigan

ON SUNDAY, June 29, 1913, at about sunset, persons in and around the horse racing track in Lansing, Michigan, were treated to an unexpected spectacle in the heavens above – a fast moving, cylindrical aerial object that zoomed across the sky going from south to north before suddenly veering off to the northwest and climbing in altitude.

An account in the *Lansing (Michigan) State Journal* said, "So swiftly did the strange craft travel that it was not more than three minutes from the time it was sighted southeast of the city until it had passed from the vision in the northwest. The aerial

EARLY 20th CENTURY UFOs

mystery carried no lights of any description and was too elongated for an ordinary balloon, it is said."

Typical Racing Track of the Early 20th Century (Wikimedia)

The newspaper article goes on to speculate that the object was either an "airship" or a "very fast traveling balloon." However, there were no known airships in the area, and a gas-filled balloon could not possibly move as fast as what the witnesses described. It remains a puzzling mystery to this day exactly what the mysterious object that buzzed Lansing, Michigan, was.

The craft "passed over Lansing about sunset Sunday evening and created some little excitement owing to the mystery surrounding the aircraft. The object appeared in the southeast and was first sighted a mile south of the race track. The craft travelled swiftly though the air, taking a direct course north until it had reached about the central

AMERICAN SIGHTINGS: 1900-1919

western part of the city when it altered its course to the northwest."

JUNE 30, 1913

Strange Aircraft Passes Over Lansing at Great Rate of Speed Sunday

What is thought to have been either an airship or a very fast traveling balloon passed over Lansing about sunset Sunday evening and created some little excitement owing to the mystery surrounding the aircraft. The object appeared in the southeast and was first sighted a mile south of the race track. The craft traveled swiftly through the air, taking a direct course north until it had reached about the central western part of the city when it altered its course to the northwest.

So swiftly did the strange craft travel that it was not more than three minutes from the time it was sighted southeast of the city until it had passed from the vision in the northwest. The aerial mystery carried no lights of any description and was too elongated for an ordinary balloon, it is said. The craft was at a great height and when it passed to the northwest of the city had reached a still higher altitude.

Lansing (Michigan) State Journal, June 30, 1913, p. 3

EARLY 20th CENTURY UFOs

Image of Lansing, Michigan, in 1909 (Library of Congress)

In this sighting, there are three points that indicate the object in the sky was something out of the ordinary:

1) The object's straight course from south to north with a sudden change to the northwest,
2) The object's "very fast" speed that took it all the way across town in three minutes, and
3) The strange shape of the object, being "too elongated for an ordinary balloon."

Unfortunately, the historical record does not contain any other accounts of "strange aircraft" in the United States in June of 1913. Therefore, this incident must continue being regarded as an unsolved mystery.

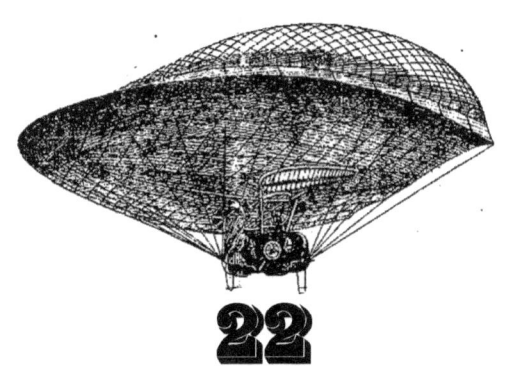

22
PROSPECTORS AND ALIENS
July 1913
Badlands, Montana

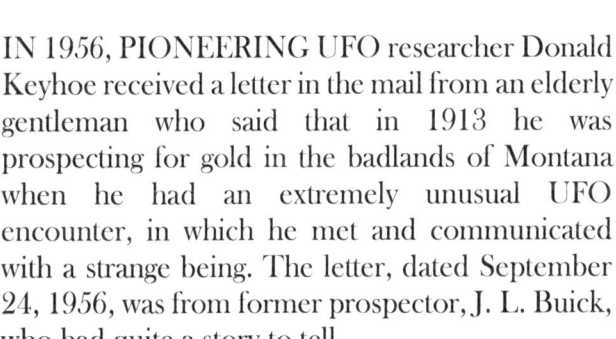

IN 1956, PIONEERING UFO researcher Donald Keyhoe received a letter in the mail from an elderly gentleman who said that in 1913 he was prospecting for gold in the badlands of Montana when he had an extremely unusual UFO encounter, in which he met and communicated with a strange being. The letter, dated September 24, 1956, was from former prospector, J. L. Buick, who had quite a story to tell.

Buick's story was also chosen by UFO researcher Ted Bloecher for inclusion in his 1979 publication "The Humanoid Catalog," which compiled significant entity encounters of the 20th century.

EARLY 20th CENTURY UFOs

Back in July 1913, Buick and another prospector were looking for gold in Montana when they suddenly became aware of another "person" standing near them.

Prospecting for Gold (Library of Congress)

A small humanoid dressed in brown had appeared among them totally undetected. The startled prospectors stood in fright, looking at the creature, when suddenly the humanoid, undoubtedly sensing their uneasiness, spoke to them in seemingly perfect English, "Peace be with you, my friends."

Words do matter, and the creature's greeting is extremely significant in terms of its historical significance. According to Daniel Esparza of *Aleteia.org*: "Certainly, the liturgical use of the classic Latin salutation *pax vobis* ('peace to you') or *pax vobiscum* ('peace be with you'), with which early Christians used to greet each other, has a

AMERICAN SIGHTINGS: 1900-1919

deep spiritual meaning. This is the classic greeting one finds in most epistles in the New Testament (Paul's, Peter's, and John's) as well as in John's Revelation. Moreover, Christ himself uses this very same salutation formula four times after his Resurrection, according to the gospels of Luke and John."

It seems clear that the humanoid intended these words to dispel the tension that had been created by its sudden appearance in the prospecting camp. Looking around to see where the creature might have come from, Buick, noticed a short distance away a silvery, round UFO that had earlier landed softly on the sandy ground without the men having detected the landing at all. The airship was nearly 100 feet in diameter, had a domed structure at its center, and also had a small "conning" tower, which is a raised platform like that found on naval vessels. Buick noted that the UFO had no "wheels," confirming that it was not a land vehicle. As Buick looked toward the ship, he noticed several other "small men," dressed in brown, exactly like the humanoid that had approached the prospectors. What especially drew Buick's attention, though, was what these little people were doing around the ship.

Some of the humanoids were examining the local vegetation and "picking flowers." Others were collecting samples of the rocks and pebbles strewn around the area. A third group of the strange visitors was engaged in "mining" a nearby outcropping of rock.

EARLY 20th CENTURY UFOs

P.T. Barnum (left) and one of the Little People in his show, c. 1862.

Turning his attention back to the first humanoid, Buick listened as the creature spoke to him again. It explained that the little people were from "another planet." Possibly realizing that the prospectors wondered how it could speak the

AMERICAN SIGHTINGS: 1900-1919

English language, the humanoid explained that its people had been "spying" on Earth for over a hundred years. The creature added that their spies were still on the Earth, disguised as circus performers. The presumption is that, because of their diminutive size, they could hide in plain sight among the show business "midgets," as they were called then, who worked in circuses.

After this exchange, the little creatures boarded their spaceship, which rose silently and was quickly gone. The amazed prospectors were left to wonder many things, it is certain. They were also possibly relieved their strange encounter was over.

Their sense of relief only lasted until the following day, when they noticed the same flying ship approaching and landing near them. This time, after the strangers again met with them, the men were offered a tour of the inside of the airship!

When the two prospectors stepped inside the ship, they saw five "concentric saucers [chambers] with diminishing air pressures, the outermost being evacuated," according to Buick.

During their tour of the ship, the prospectors were told that the spacecraft achieved propulsion through the manipulation of gravity. Their hosts said, "Gravity is only a different type of magnetism," and added that gravity can be controlled and manipulated by an electromagnetic drive. Using this motive force, they were told, the flying ship could achieve speeds of 9,000 miles per hour. Such power was totally superior to the use of rockets, which had been tried but discarded.

EARLY 20th CENTURY UFOs

13-01　July, 1913　Badlands area, Montana　　　　　　　　Type G

J. L. Buick & another prospector were startled by a small brown man saying "Peace be with you, my friends." Sitting on a patch of sand was a silvery round object nearly 100 ft in diameter, with central dome & a small conning tower; no wheels underneath. Around it were other small men in brown picking flowers, pebbles, &c., & some mining a rock outcrop. The occupant told the witnesses they were from another planet which had secretly been keeping tabs on earth for over a hundred years; they had learned English via spies working in a U.S. circus. The craft rose silently & then took off. Next day it came back, & they were given a tour inside: 5 concentric saucers with diminishing air pressures, the outermost being evacuated. As to lift, "gravity is only a different type of magnetism", so it can be controlled by an electromagnetic drive; they can do 9000 mph, and have artificial gravity inside the saucer. Rockets, they were told, had failed for space travel.

Investigator:

Source: Witness's letter of 9/24/56 to Donald Keyhoe.

Notes from the Buick Interview (NICAP)

AMERICAN SIGHTINGS: 1900-1919

The strangers also stated that their ship was equipped with "artificial gravity," which made it convenient to move around during space flight.

In the end, though the story is fascinating, clearly there is insufficient data now existing regarding the original eyewitness and his testimony. Unfortunately, the historical record does not seem to contain any information about a person named "J. L. Buick," who prospected for gold in Montana in 1913. Since a span of 39 years had passed before Buick sent his letter to Donald Keyhoe and assuming he had been in his 20s when prospecting, the witness would likely have been in his 60s or 70s in 1952.

Donald E. Keyhoe

Unfortunately, the information gathered by Keyhoe, and later Bloecher, contains very little about Buick that could be useful in confirming his identity and verifying that he was in Montana at the time he claimed he was. Also, no mention is made of the identity of the other prospector that was working with him.

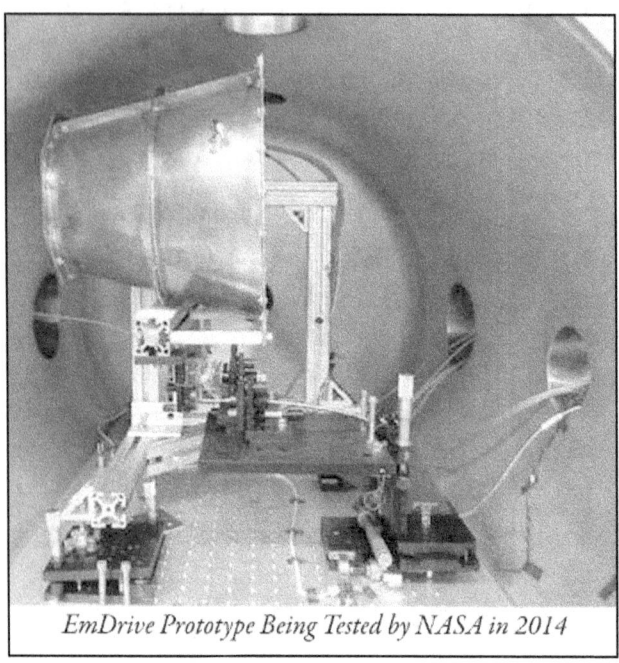

EmDrive Prototype Being Tested by NASA in 2014

In summary, we have a very compelling story that appears to be plausible and that contains a number of very interesting details. Unfortunately, confirmation of the data presented is not possible. We leave the reader with one final, interesting tidbit. The small humanoids explained to Buick that their ship used an "electromagnetic drive" to navigate through space. Interestingly, such a drive for propelling spacecraft was actually designed in 2001 and prototypes have now been developed and are being tested by a number of research teams, including one from NASA. The so-called

AMERICAN SIGHTINGS: 1900-1919

"EmDrive" works by converting electricity into microwaves and channeling this electromagnetic radiation through a conical chamber. In theory, the microwaves can exert force against the walls of the chamber to produce enough thrust to propel a spacecraft through outer space. It's not quite "anti-gravity," but it seems to have some design similarities to the drive that was mentioned to Buick by the humanoids back in 1913.

Just in case you were tempted to scoff at the "tall tale" spun by two Montana prospectors, you might want to wait to see what happens with the development of this revolutionary new spacecraft propulsion system that appears to have first been shown to us in 1913!

EARLY 20th CENTURY UFOs

Photo of Marine Band Harmonica (Pixabay)

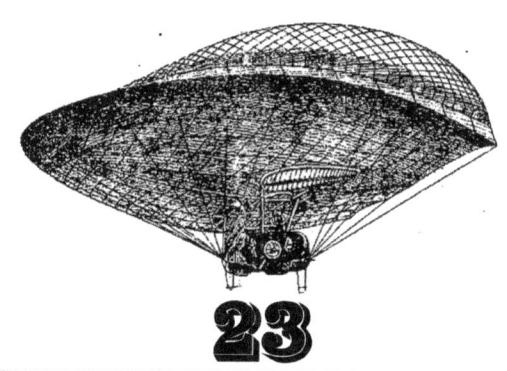

23
ALIEN MUSIC
1914
Pawtucket, Rhode Island

IN 1982, LEGENDARY U.S. astronomer and UFO researcher J. Allen Hynek received a letter from Hans M. Schnitzler, a 75-year-old retiree living in Flagler Beach, Florida, disclosing an amazing UFO encounter that he had in 1914, during which he heard a haunting melody. Along with the letter, Hynek received a cassette tape recording of Schnitzler using a harmonica to recreate the "music" he heard during his UFO experience.

Hynek had Schnitzler's letter published in the December 1982 / January 1983 newsletter of the

Center for UFO Studies (CUFOS), of which Hynek was the director. In addition, Hynek made copies of Schnitzler's cassette tape available to researchers wanting to hear it.

Dr. J. Allen Hynek (left) and Dr. Jacques Vallée (right), circa 1978

In his letter to Hynek, Schnitzler opened by saying that although the UFO encounter happened when he was eight years old, "what I saw definitely was a space vehicle." He added, "From what I saw, there is no doubt in my mind that there are alien or friendly people from outer space."

He commented that he decided to come forward with his story after a friend of his told him of a UFO sighting that he had just experienced. That caused Schnitzler to recall what happened in his childhood and created a desire to finally disclose it publicly.

AMERICAN SIGHTINGS: 1900-1919

Born in New York City on December 2, 1906, Schnitzler would have turned eight in December 1914. Although he gives no date for his encounter, he did say he was eight years old at the time, which suggests it probably happened around the latter part of the year. At the time of the experience, he and his family were living in Pawtucket, Rhode Island.

"One Sunday afternoon, my parents, sister and I were out walking down toward the Blackstone River. On the way, we passed a trash dump where I spotted an old pendulum clock. I wanted to take it home, but my father forbade it. But the next day, returning home from school, I went back to the dump, picked up the clock and took it home, sitting on our lawn with it, between our home and a low picket fence, this was about 3 p.m."

Giving context to the location, Schnitzler added, "Across the street there was a little white church with granite posts surrounding it and iron pipes running through them."

His odd encounter then ensued, beginning with a strange sound. "Suddenly, I heard a musical humming sound. At first, I thought it was the clock. I turned my head and there it [the UFO] was across the street in front of the church about 25 feet from me."

His description of the ship was incredibly detailed for an event that had occurred 68 years earlier: "The spacecraft hovered over the fence and partially over the street about 10 feet above the ground. According to my recollection, it was about 30 feet wide and about 10 feet high. It stayed there motionless. The ship, I believe, was gray in color. It had a gradual dome on top with a sharp radius coming down to a flat. The dome was about two-thirds the width of it. The bottom was slightly domed with a sharper radius going to the outer edge. The center of the dome, I thought, was about one half of the total height."

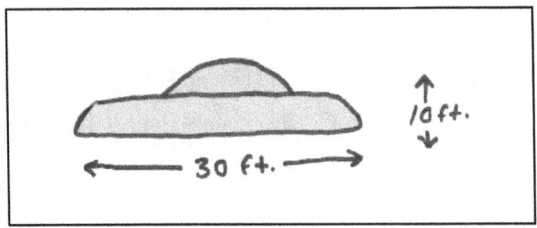

As Schnitzler stared in amazement, he saw an opening suddenly appear in the hull of the ship. "As I watched, an opening appeared like two convoluted sliding doors from the center out, making an opening about four feet wide. Two little people walked out and filed to each side of the door, walking on the flat of the ship, then two more etc., until there were eight abreast."

His initial impression of the humanoids was that they were children, but their heads appeared rounder than normal human heads. "At the time, I thought they were children. I remembered they had arms and legs. The shape of their heads, I believe, were round but their faces I can't recall."

It was at this time in the sighting that the singing began - a haunting melody that stayed with Schnitzler for the rest of his life. He said, "Then suddenly, they sang in beautiful harmony. Yes gentlemen, they sang loud and clear a melody over

AMERICAN SIGHTINGS: 1900–1919

and over again as if they wanted me to familiarize myself with it." It was this strange, beautiful music that Schnitzler later tried to recapture with his harmonica in the cassette tape he sent to J. Allen Hynek in 1982.

When the unearthly recital was completed, the UFO occupants moved, in a very orderly manner, back into their ship. "When they stopped singing, the doors opened again, and they all filed back into the ship in the same order." The spaceship then lifted up and, very slowly, moved up into the sky over the church and was soon lost to view.

Highly puzzled after such a strange encounter, the eight-year-old sought out the advice of his parent. At the supper table that evening, he recounted his encounter briefly and asked his parents, "What is an automobile without wheels doing, going up into the air?"

Pausing her meal, his mother replied in her native German, "You must have been dreaming."

Later in the evening, after Schnitzler had gone to his upstairs bedroom, he heard his dad speaking about his own father's UFO experience, which had taken place in the Black Forest in Germany and was similar to what Schnitzler had witnessed.

In the letter to Hynek, Schnitzler explained that his father bought him a Marine Band harmonica when he was seven years old, and he had learned to play it. After the UFO encounter, he taught himself to play the melody that he had heard the "little people" singing. He played it for his mother, but she said that she had never heard it before.

EARLY 20th CENTURY UFOs

Schnitzler concluded his letter by writing, "Gentlemen, from my experience and encounter with these little space people, I feel they are kind and tolerant. I asked myself why would they sing to a lonesome boy who could not mingle with other children because of a language barrier? Perhaps they understood."

He added, "This memory has brought emotional feelings over me many times. I just had to write and tell you people because I am sure you will understand and believe me. To me, it was the most wonderful experience I can remember other than my wife and children."

Explaining why he decided to contact CUFOS, Schnitzler said, "I read about your organization in our local paper and truly believe we are not alone in this great world of ours."

Six years after sharing his experience with J. Allen Hynek, Hans Schnitzler died, on August 20, 1988, at the age of 81. His obituary, appearing in the August 21, 1988 edition of the *Orlando Sentinel*, stated that he had worked as a tool and die maker for Texas Instruments. To our knowledge, he disclosed no further information about his encounter, and the current whereabouts of his cassette tape recording are unknown.

Did it really happen? Schnitzler certainly seemed to believe it, and it impacted his life in a powerful way until the very end. As he was close to the end of his life when he disclosed the experience, it seems unlikely that he had any ulterior motives, such as profit or publicity, for coming forward.

24
MYSTERIOUS LOW FLYING UFO

February 9, 1916
Bigfork, Montana

AT 5 IN THE MORNING on Tuesday, February 9, 1916, a huge, blimp-like object was seen flying low and moving from southeast to northwest over the town of Bigfork, Montana.

Among those who saw it was Bigfork resident Charles Russell who heard a loud "buzzing noise" coming from the sky above him. Turning to look up, he saw a "huge black mass" floating just above his garage. It was "not very high in the air." Bright moonlight enabled Russell to get a good look at the object as it passed overhead.

EARLY 20th CENTURY UFOs

STRANGE AIRSHIP WORRIES FLATHEAD

Polson, Feb. 14.—(Special.)—The passage of an airship last Tuesday over Big Fork and the upper end of Flathead lake is reported by Charles Russell, who lives near that place. Mr. Russell says that at about 5 o'clock in the morning he heard a loud buzzing noise over his head and looking up saw a huge black mass just over his garage building and not very high in the air. He says it was headed in a northwesterly direction and went out over the lake. Mr. Russell says it was moonlight at the time but that the machine passed from sight in a few minutes. A good many have expressed the opinion that the aircraft was from Canada.

The Whitefish Pilot reports that an airship of the gas-bag type passed over the city about the same hour on Tuesday morning.

SOURCE:
The Missoulian
(Missoula, Montana)
Feb 15, 1915, Page 5

Newspaper Article About the Sighting

As the strange object moved away from above his property, it kept heading to the northwest over Flathead Lake. The entire duration of the sighting was only a few minutes, according to Russell. After moving over the lake, the craft soon disappeared from view.

A newspaper article about the sighting appeared in the February 15, 1915 edition of the *Missoulian* titled "Strange Airship Worries Flathead." After describing what Russell saw, the article states that many people in the area were expressing the opinion that the "aircraft" was from Canada, although no explanation is given as to why this theory was prevalent.

AMERICAN SIGHTINGS: 1900-1919

*Flathead Lake, Near Bigfork, Montana
(Katie Brady, CC BY-SA 2.0,)*
https://commons.wikimedia.org/w/index.php?curid=4834147

The article also states, "The *Whitefish Pilot* reports that an airship of the gas-bag type passed over the city about the same hour on Tuesday morning." The town of Whitefish is located about 50 miles north-northwest of Bigfork, which means that it could have been the same object that was seen in both places.

To provide context on this sighting, an article in the *Butte (Montana) Miner* newspaper pointed out that the area had experienced a series of similar sightings of "mysterious movements by aeroplanes" for about a week prior to Russell's sighting.

"Airships have been reported as hovering above Polson, Bigfork, and other towns, and by farmers on the prairie. No one in this section is known to own an airship, and the identity of the airmen and their purpose."

EARLY 20th CENTURY UFOs

SEE AIRSHIP ON FLATHEAD RESERVE

Missoula, Feb. 15.—Flathead reservation points report mysterious movements by aeroplanes within the past week. Airships have been reported as hovering above Polson, Big Fork and other towns, and by farmers on the prairie. No one in this section is known to own an airship and the identity of the airmen and their purpose.

The Butte (Montana) Miner, Feb. 15, 1915, Page 1

The sightings around Flathead Lake, Montana, remain unexplained to this day. Might the craft seen have been man-made or were they something else? We may never know for certain

A Typical Dirigible (Circa 1919)

25
UFO OVER LAKE SUPERIOR

February 29, 1916
Superior, Wisconsin

AT 4:30 IN THE MORNING on February 29, 1916, several late-night shift workers on the shores of Lake Superior in Michigan and at nearby Duluth, Minnesota, received the shock of their lives. Dock workers in Superior were going through their normal early morning duties when they suddenly saw an immense UFO appear before them, hovering over the lake.

The witnesses later stated that the object was a "big machine 50 feet wide and 100 feet long" with three bright lights, one at each end and another in the middle. It appeared that the machine was dangling a long rope or cable beneath it.

EARLY 20th CENTURY UFOs

MYSTERIOUS AIR SHIP STIRS DULUTH POLICE

Trails Heavy Object at End of Long Rope.

Machine Is of Gigantic Size, Carries Red and Green Lights and Has Wings Numbered.

Duluth, Minn., Feb. 29.—Following reports today that the mysterious aeroplane that has been hovering over Duluth and Superior was again seen last night, Commissioner Silberstein, head of the Duluth safety division, announced that instructions will be given the police to be on the lookout for the air machine. That an aeroplane really is flying over the American head of the lakes during the early hours of the morning, is admitted by police here and in Superior.

Three men were aboard the big plane today when it was seen over Superior. A long rope with some heavy object on the end of it is hanging from the machine, eye witnesses say.

The Topeka (Kansas) Daily Capital, 3-1-1916, p. 3

AMERICAN SIGHTINGS: 1900-1919

*Docks in the Lake Superior Region
(Detroit Publishing Co. / Public domain)*

The witnesses stated that they saw three "pilots" inside the UFO and that they heard noises as if from an engine.

Investigator T. Peter Park, in a 2003 article titled "February 1916 Lake Superior Mystery Aeroplanes," wrote: "Five watchmen at the Globe Elevators, the Great Northern Elevator, and the Carnegie Coal Dock on Superior's St. Louis River waterfront saw an 'aeroplane' with three lights carrying three passengers fly from east to west over the docks and elevators between 4:30 and 4:45 a.m. on the morning of Tuesday, February 29, 1916. The witnesses heard 'roaring' or 'purring' engine noises coming from the sky, and saw a big 'aeroplane' with three lights and three 'men'

EARLY 20th CENTURY UFOs

aboard, at a height of 600 to 1,000 feet in the air, trailing a long rope or cable with a large block or object at the end, heading up the St. Louis River and vanishing to the west. John Gustavson, watchman at the Carnegie Coal Dock, estimated its altitude at 1,000 feet and added that he had thought news reports of people seeing an 'aeroplane' at Allouez and other places were a 'joke,' until he himself saw the craft at 4:35 that morning. John Tullyson, head watchman at Globe Elevators, described the 'aeroplane' as 'flying along very fast' with a 'roaring noise' about 4:30, and estimated altitude at about 600 feet. He described it as 50 feet wide and 100 feet long, with three lights, one at each end and one in the middle. He saw one of the three 'men' sitting near the front of the machine, 'probably running it,' the other two a little behind him and seemingly 'looking around.' Two other Globe Elevator night watchmen did not see the machine which had disappeared behind an elevator but heard its engine noise. A night watchman at the Great Northern Elevator who wished to remain anonymous heard a 'purring noise in the sky' about 4:30 or 4:45 and saw an 'aeroplane' passing over to the west, with 3 lights 'of a sort of reddish color.'"

As is the case with a lot of UFO sightings and encounters, skeptics stepped in with an alternate explanation for what the dock workers claimed to have seen. It was widely reported that a "toy balloon carrying three lights" was to blame for the sighting.

AMERICAN SIGHTINGS: 1900-1919

> **SUPERIOR STILL CLAIMS TO HAVE SEEN AEROPLANE**
>
> SUPERIOR, Wis., March 3.—Employees at the Great Northern ore docks and at the Carnegie coal dock on Thursday continued to insist that they had really seen an aeroplane and many Superior residents are unwilling to believe that toy balloons explain the mysterious object seen soaring over the city. They called attention to the fact that the machine disappeared in the west. According to official records of the weather department, this would have been impossible had the object been a toy balloon, as the wind was from that direction and blowing a stiff gale, too.

The Journal Times (Racine, WI), March 3, 1916, page 2.

However, the original witnesses did not budge from their initial statement. The newspaper *Journal-News* of Racine, Wisconsin, reported on March 3, 1916: "Employees at the Great Northern Ore docks and at the Carnegie coal dock on Thursday continued to insist that they had really seen an aeroplane and many Superior residents are unwilling to believe that toy balloons explain the mysterious object seen soaring over the city. They called attention to the fact that the machine disappeared in the west. According to official records of the weather department, this would have been impossible had the object been a toy balloon, as the wind was from that direction and blowing a stiff gale, too."

Man-made Aeroplane (Circa 1912)

Because of the claims that what the witnesses saw were actually toy balloons made of paper, many UFO researchers have dismissed this episode as a hoax. However, serious questions remain, including the huge size of the object seen (up to 100 feet in length), the three humanoid figures seen inside the craft, the three bright lights on the object, the "roaring" engine noise, and the fast speed at which the object traveled.

It is also noteworthy that the airplanes of 1916 do not seem to fit the description of what the dock workers saw flying over Lake Superior. These early airplanes were very primitive, usually carried only one or two persons, often had no lights on them, had a very obvious propeller, mostly flew in daytime, and did not travel very fast.

*A Weather Balloon in the 1940s
(U.S. Navy Photo)*

Researchers acknowledge that the sightings of "mystery aeroplanes" over Michigan and Minnesota in February 1916 (during World War I) caused much panic and alarm among the local population. It was to the advantage of local authorities to allay fears and calm the panic, perhaps by introducing a story of "toy balloons" being to blame for the mysterious sightings. This is a strategy that government has adopted to try to explain away other UFO sightings such as the 1947 Roswell UFO incident, where a "weather balloon" was blamed for what witnesses saw.

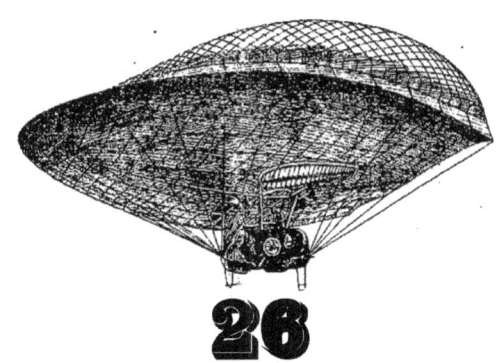

26
MULTIPLE UFOS OVER COLORADO
September 1917
Salida, Colorado

ON SEPTEMBER 7, 1917, the *Salida (Colorado) Record* published an amazing account of mysterious "vehicles of the air" that flew over town every evening for an entire week and were seen by hundreds of witnesses.

Residents of Salida observed lights moving through the night sky, in various parts of the heavens. They would appear for an instant, disappear, and then reappear stronger than ever, before again vanishing. The objects did not seem to be close to the observers, but rather seemed quite distant.

EARLY 20th CENTURY UFOs

Salida, Colorado in 1894 (Courtesy Salida Regional Library)

Reverend George M. Oakley of the Presbyterian Church, described by the newspaper as a "pillar of Salida society," examined one of the objects through a telescope and could see what looked like a "wheel" about three feet in diameter. "While the wheel seemed to revolve, vari-colored lights appeared. Without the telescope, the light appeared to be about the size of a croquet ball as compared with the stars."

The lights were seen to the north of town, over Tenderfoot Mountain, and above Mt. Shavano, appearing to be at great distances.

The newspaper account stated that the aerial visitors were certainly not airplanes because airplanes do not have the appearance of a revolving wheel. Neither could they have been any sort of dirigible, and there were no known aviation fields in Colorado in 1917.

AMERICAN SIGHTINGS: 1900-1919

Tenderfoot Mountain
(Courtesy Salida Regional Library)

The article concluded by saying, "Is it then some genius who has discovered some new principle of flight and is trying out his invention? It's your guess. What is it?"

The sightings were also mentioned briefly by the other newspaper in town, the *Salida Mail*, in an article on the same day, September 7, 1917. The *Mail* mentioned that the lights were also seen by National Guard soldiers at camp in Pueblo, Colorado. The young men at the camp were "all in good spirits, but the principal excitement was over the nightly appearance of an unusual light, which is suspected of being a new style of air craft. The light also has been seen in Salida by several people and opinion is divided as to whether it is the Pike's Peak searchlight or a strange flyer. Some of the Salida observers say the light is of various hues and appears in different parts of the skies. Some saw the light in two places at the same time."

EARLY 20th CENTURY UFOs

A number of Salida residents who witnessed the strange objects were identified in the *Salida Record*. Among them were Carl F. Bode (1868-1948), a locomotive engineer for the railroad, and his family, whose identities were confirmed via the 1920 U.S. Census and a number of other sources. Also named was Mr. Franklin Cicero Woody (1862-1926), a cashier at the "National Bank," and his wife Louise.

But the most prominent eyewitness was the Reverend George M. Oakley and his wife. Oakley had come to Salida in May 1916 after being pastor of the Presbyterian churches in Huntington, Tennessee, and Weatherford, Texas.

Oakley developed health problems due to Salida's altitude and was advised to relocate to a lower altitude. He left Salida in July 1919, to become pastor of the Presbyterian church in Jackson, Tennessee. Upon the announcement of his departure, the *Salida Mail* newspaper, on June 27, 1919, said "Mr. Oakley is a gifted speaker and an enthusiastic worker. He took an active interest in every movement for the betterment of the city and was honored with the leadership of many important campaigns. He was appointed chairman of the two Red Cross drives, chairman of the two YMCA drives, and chairman of the United War Work drive, all of which went over the top, two of them doubling the quota. He took an active interest in the work of the Red Cross chapter and was at the head of several important committees of that organization during the war. Mr. Oakley is popular, not only with the members of his own congregation but with the entire citizenry."

LOOK ONCE! LOOK TWICE! SEE IT? AIRSHIP OR AIRSHIPS SPY US

E. C. Newby and Cal Brown motored to Pueblo Sunday to visit the Salida boys at Camp Gunter, returning yesterday. They declared the boys were all in good spirits but the principal excitement was over the nightly appearance of an unusual light, which is suspected of being a new style of air craft.

The light also has been seen in Salida by several people and opinion is divided as to whether it is the Pike's Peak searchlight or a strange flyer.

Some of the Salida observers say the light is of various hues and appears in different parts of the skies.

Some saw the light in two places at the same time, which is a reminder of the sea yarn about the old ship captain who was sitting in a tavern by the seashore drinking with his son. He cautioned his son about drinking too much and remarked that it was easy to tell when he had too much because objects appeared double.

"For instance" said the captain, looking over the bay, "there are two masts yonder. Now, if I should see four masts, I would know it was time for me to stop drinking."

"But Father," interrupted the youth "I see only one mast."

The boys at Camp Gunter are excited over the coming execution of a cook, who was convicted by a court martial of having attempted to poison the butter served to the soldiers. He is to be shot at sunrise, but the date is not known to the men. A firing squad of six men of whom two will have loaded rifles, will execute the sentence of death, according to the statement made to Mr. Newby by the men.

From the Salida (Colorado) Mail, Sept. 7, 1917, p. 1

The incident was largely forgotten until Salida had another fascinating UFO incident on August 27, 1995. Restaurant owner Timothy Everett Edwards (1953-2008) captured on video a strange, flattened disc UFO in the sky over Salida. His video was eventually shown on numerous television programs, including *Sightings*. After Edwards filmed his famous footage, researchers looking at previous UFO cases in Salida rediscovered the 1917 event, which was briefly

EARLY 20th CENTURY UFOs

featured in a number of newspaper and magazine articles released in 1995.

The 1917 case is a fascinating sighting indeed from the early 20th century. It occurred in an area with no known aviation, was seen by multiple, reliable witnesses over a one-week period, and was never explained. As such, we should place it firmly in the category of a confirmed UFO sighting.

CLOSE ENCOUNTER IN PENNSYLVANIA

October 1917
Youngstown, Pennsylvania

IN HIS 1963 BOOK *A Carbon Experiment*, Indiana UFO researcher Orvil R. Hartle first disclosed the story of an amazing flying saucer encounter that occurred in Youngstown, Pennsylvania, in October 1917. Hartle was a member of the National Investigations Committee on Aerial Phenomena (NICAP), serving as chairman of the LaPorte, Indiana, chapter.

The UFO encounter involving the sighting of entities occurred shortly after midnight on an unknown date in October 1917 in Youngstown, Pennsylvania, a borough in Westmoreland

County. Youngstown is located about 45 miles east-southeast of Pittsburgh.

Typical Locomotive of 1916 (Public Domain)

The eyewitness was 17-year-old John Boback, whose identity has been confirmed via the 1920 U.S. Census. Born in Galicia, near Spain, in 1900, Baback was a mine worker residing in the nearby unincorporated area known as South Union.

According to his eyewitness account, the young man was walking along the railroad tracks between Youngstown and Mount Braddock, when he suddenly encountered a saucer-shaped craft with a landing platform of some type and having rows of lights along its hull. He observed the object, which was sitting in a pasture about 100 feet off to his left, for one to two minutes, noticing that it was about the size of a standard automobile of the time – about 20 feet in diameter. On top of the object was a dome with elongated windows, through which Boback could see silhouetted humanoid "figures" inside the vehicle.

AMERICAN SIGHTINGS: 1900-1919

As Boback continued to view the craft, he noticed a high-pitched sound building up, during which the object gradually rose into the air and began moving away at a slow speed not unlike the aircraft of the time. French UFO researcher Jean Sider in his 2007 book *Les 'Extraterrestres' Avant les Soucoupes Volantes* commented, "The witness became frightened, contemplated the thing for a minute or two until the craft departed by gradually rising slowly like an airplane, emitting a high-pitched sound."

Similar Domed Saucer

Especially intriguing about this case is the fact that a metallic saucer-shaped object with humanoid figures inside was encountered by a witness long

EARLY 20th CENTURY UFOs

before the "flying saucer" craze of the 1940s and 1950s. The witness saw the ship land in a field and observed it take off.

Although no specific, detailed description is given about the humanoid "figures" seen inside the craft, most UFO reports from this time period did not include sightings of beings. The fact that the eyewitness reported seeing these "figures" is another unique characteristic of this case.

The size of the ship, 20 feet in diameter, seems particularly small, although the size is an estimate given by the eyewitness standing at a distance of about 100 feet. Other similarly small UFOs have been seen over the many years of observations.

Regarding the UFO researcher who first reported on this case, Orvil R. Hartle (1920 - 1985) was active with NICAP in the 1960s. A native of La Porte, Indiana, Hartle served in the U.S. Navy during World War II in the 31st Special Battalion Seabees. Hartle passed away in 1985 at the age of 65.

In conclusion, John Boback's 1917 close encounter in Youngstown, Pennsylvania, remains one of the most intriguing UFO sightings of the early 20th century.

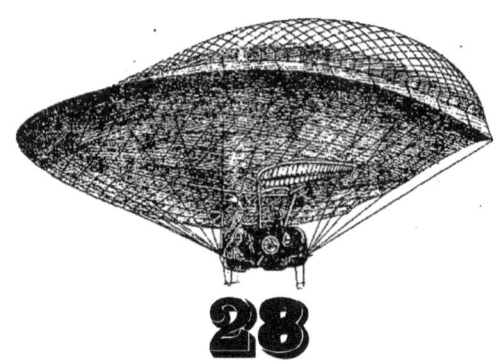

28
TEXAS SOLDIERS SEE UFO

August 21, 1918
Waco, Texas

ON AUGUST 21, 1918, Edwin Bauhan, a young flight cadet stationed at Rich Field, a World War I military airfield in Waco, Texas, reported seeing a large cigar-shaped UFO of perhaps 125 to 150 feet in diameter. The object was also witnessed by several other solders at Rich Field.

The eyewitness account was reported in Michael David Hall's 1999 book *UFOs: A Century of Sightings*: "As we were coming from the mess hall after our meal, we suddenly saw approaching the camp what seemed to be a Zeppelin at first glance. It came directly overhead and was no more than

EARLY 20th CENTURY UFOs

five hundred feet high, so we got an excellent view of it. It had no motors, no rigging and was noiseless. I knew where it was going, steering from southwest to northeast. It was not quite a rose, or sort of flame color. It could be said to be cigar shaped. I could observe no windows, though there could have been some. We all experienced the weirdest feeling of our lives and sat in our tent puzzling over it for some time. Through the years, I came to the conclusion that it was controlled from some other planet, had no one in it, and was being used as an instrument of observation."

Aircraft from Rich Field Flying Over Waco in 1918 (U.S. Army Photo)

What is most interesting in this case is that the observers were military aviators. As such, they would have been well trained at identifying the aircraft of the time. Bauhan noted that the ship appeared at first to be a "Zeppelin," although he clearly later felt that it was not a dirigible at all.

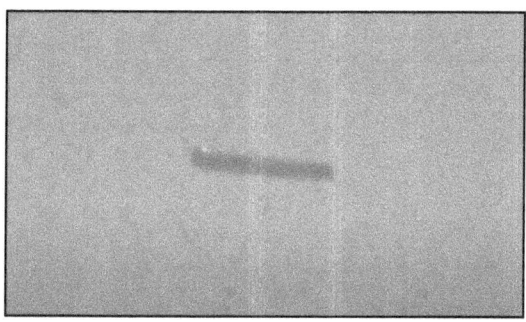

Cigar shaped UFO seen in Brazil in 2011 (YouTube)

It was a reddish cigar-shaped craft, 125-150 feet in diameter, that moved across the sky noiselessly. The ship was so unusual that Bauhan and his fellow soldiers spent quite a lot of time after the sighting trying to figure out what it was that they might have seen.

Bauhan finally concluded that the craft must have come to the Earth from another planet, because neither he nor his comrades could come up with any other more reasonable explanation. This realization obviously had a profound impact on the life of Bauhan. Unfortunately, the historical record is strangely silent about his activities later in life. One can only assume that he continued thinking about what he witnessed for the remainder of his days.

EARLY 20th CENTURY UFOs

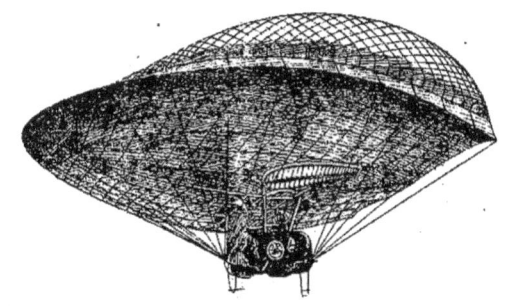

POSTSCRIPT
VIRUS FROM OUTER SPACE?
1918
New York, New York

DID A MYSTERIOUS VIRUS that struck America and the world in 1918, killing an estimated 500 million people, possibly originate in outer space? Some researchers over the years have wondered about this possibility.

The 1918 worldwide flu pandemic, sometimes called the "Spanish flu," is still a mystery in terms of where it came from. Some of the first cases were documented in February 1918 in Haskell County, Kansas, and in New York City, as well as in several places in Europe. Scientists say the pandemic, which plagued the world for at least two years, was caused by a form of the H1N1 influenza A virus

EARLY 20th CENTURY UFOs

and that it possibly originated in birds. But nobody knows for certain.

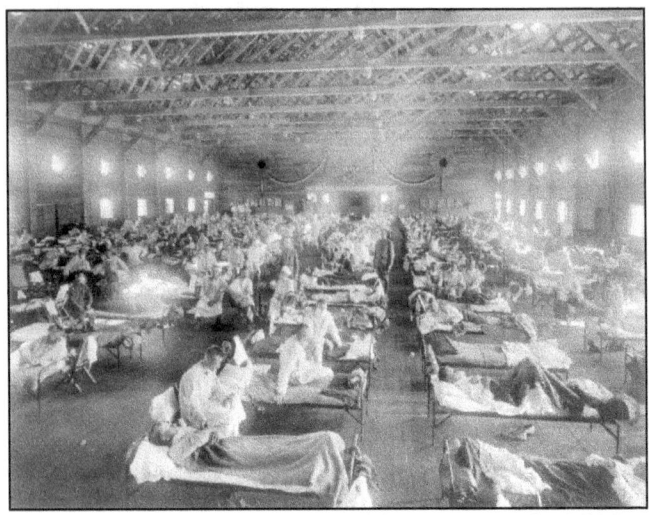

Spanish Flu Victims at Fort Riley, Kansas, in 1918 (Public Domain via Wikimedia Commons)

According to an article published in the *New York Herald* on Sunday, January 25, 1920, there were some people who entertained the possibility that the deadly pandemic may have originated in outer space. The article quoted one of the world's foremost scientists and inventors of the time, Thomas Edison, as saying, "We have no reason positively to declare that definitive influences even other than electrical have not reached us out of space. There was the Spanish influenza, so called, for example. We are not sure that it originated on this planet. It spread everywhere irrespective of the lines of human travel."

AMERICAN SIGHTINGS: 1900-1919

American Scientist Thomas Alva Edison
(Library of Congress)

Edison continued, "It has been established that it [the flu pandemic] appeared upon Pacific Ocean islands which had had no communication with any infected portion of the world; or, indeed, any portion of the world whatever. Ships reaching utterly isolated islands found half of their inhabitants ill or dead of the disease."

EARLY 20th CENTURY UFOs

Edison theorized that the pandemic might have been deposited upon the Earth from outer space, stating, "Some scientific man has said that we were passing through a cloud of benzol [benzene] vapor floating in space. Benzol is poisonous. It might affect all humanity physically; it might affect all human thought, distorting it, for it is known to have an influence on the brain."

Benzene is a natural constituent of crude oil and is a known human carcinogen. It has been linked to numerous human health problems and continues to be a major health problem today.

Interestingly, infrared astronomical studies in 1997 determined the presence of benzene in outer space.

Back in 1920, Thomas Edison wrote, "It is not unreasonable to suppose that more than once, we have passed through realms of space permeated with vapors of one kind or another. If this occurs, it is not unreasonable to expect them to affect humanity."

Interestingly, the idea that the Earth might be affected by passing through toxic particles in space was first proposed by Sir Arthur Conan Doyle in his 1913 short novel *The Poison Belt*, wherein a famous scientist accurately predicts that the planet will be adversely affected when it passes through "a belt of poisonous ether."

Conan Doyle wrote in his novel, "Deep in that ocean we are floating upon a slow current. Might that current not drift us into belts of ether which are novel and have properties of which we have never conceived? There is a change somewhere.... To take an obvious example, who would undertake to say that the mysterious and universal outbreak of illness, recorded in your columns this very morning as having broken out among the indigenous races of Sumatra, has no connection with some cosmic change to which they may respond more quickly than the more complex peoples of Europe?"

Sir Arthur Conan Doyle (Public Domain)

EARLY 20th CENTURY UFOs

So, did the 1918 flu pandemic originate in outer space? We may never know for certain, but even as these words are being written, in June of 2020, the world is again in the grips of another horrible pandemic whose origins are still somewhat unexplained. Are there forces at work, possibly extraterrestrial, conspiring to keep our planet's burgeoning population under control?

INDEX

A Princess of Mars, 75
alien beings
   as giants, 205
   as greys, 164, 176
   as humanoids, 90, 100
   as little green men, 152
   as luminous beings, 33, 39
   as Martians, 78
   as tall humanoids, 42, 45, 61
   described as being pigeon-like, 120
Anaconda, Montana, 29
Beesley, Lawrence, 138, 141
Bloecher, Ted, 119, 163
Bridgewater, Massachusetts, 107
Burlington, Vermont, 101
Chupacabra, 15
Conan Doyle, Sir Arthur, 208
Crone, Lawrence, 122, 125
Denton, William, 74-75
Dickson, Tennessee, 89
Edison, Thomas, 12, 206, 208
Farmersville, Texas, 151-153
Ford, Idella, 129-132
Fort Worth, Texas, 145
Fort, Charles, 143-144, 148
Gollywogs, 65

Hall, Michael David, 201
Hartle, Orvil R., 197
Hill, Betty and Barney, 127
Hynek, J. Allen, 129, 132, 134, 151, 173-174, 177-178
Imperial Valley, California, 113
Iola, Kansas, 41-44
Keyhoe, Donald, 47, 145, 148, 163, 169
Lake Ontario, 70
Lake Superior, 183-188
Lake Tinsel, Alaska, 61
Lansing, Michigan, 159-162
Latham, Silbie, 151-153
Leyson, Sackville Gwyn, 73-81
Marconi, Guglielmo, 26
Mars, 23, 26-28, 73-81
NASA, 77, 170
Pawtucket, Rhode Island, 175
Philadelphia Experiment, The, 53-58
Piqua, Ohio, 129
Pueblo, Colorado, 12, 193
RMS Titanic, 136-142
Rochester, New York, 67
Salida, Colorado, 192
Salton Sea, 113-117
San Francisco, California, 47
Sider, Jean, 199

EARLY 20th CENTURY UFOs

Spanish flu, 204-209
Tesla, Nikola, 20-28
U.S. Weather Bureau, 47, 68
unidentified flying object
    as airship, 83, 100, 113, 117, 179
    as cylindrical object, 102, 120, 159, 202
    as flying saucer, 176, 198
    as luminous object, 15, 18, 29, 32, 55, 138, 191
    as meteors, 49, 52, 67
    as mothership, 148
USS Eldridge, 53-58
Van Meter, Iowa, 34-39
Venus, 23, 28
Violetville, Maryland, 119-120
Waco, Texas, 201
Wilmington, Vermont, 17
Woodbury, Urban A., 101
Wright Brothers, 10
Youngstown, Pennsylvania, 197, 200

ABOUT THE AUTHOR

Noe Torres is a recognized expert in the field of UFOs and the paranormal. He is an author, publisher, and member of the Mutual UFO Network (MUFON). He holds a Bachelor's in English and a Master's in Library Science from the University of Texas at Austin. He has written one of the most popular books about the famous Roswell Incident, titled *Ultimate Guide to the Roswell UFO Crash*, which is the top selling book among tourists visiting Roswell, New Mexico. He has also written several other well-reviewed books, including *Mexico's Roswell*, *The Other Roswell*, *Aliens in the Forest*, *Fallen Angel*, and *The Coyame Incident*.

Noe has appeared on several nationally-broadcast television shows, including season 2, episode 1 of the Travel Channel's *Mysteries of the Outdoors*, titled "Strange Attraction," which premiered in August 2017. In that show, he is interviewed extensively about unexplained mysteries in Big Bend National Park. Also, in 2017, Noe was featured in an episode titled "The Marfa Lights" for the TV series *Mysteries of the Unexplained*. In 2008, he appeared in season 1, episode 4 of the

History Channel's *UFO Hunters*, in a show called "Crash and Retrieval."

Noe has appeared several times on George Noory's famous radio show *Coast to Coast AM*, as well as on The Jeff Rense Program and may other shows. He is also in high demand as a speaker at UFO and paranormal conferences and festivals, having been a featured speaker at the 2017 International UFO Congress in Scottsdale, Arizona. He has also spoken five times at the annual Roswell UFO Conference and at many other UFO conferences throughout the United States and Mexico.

ABOUT THE AUTHOR

John LeMay was born and raised in Roswell, NM, the "UFO Capital of the World." He is the author of over 25 books on film and western history such as *Kong Unmade: The Lost Films of Skull Island*, *Tall Tales and Half Truths of Billy the Kid*, and *Roswell USA: Towns That Celebrate UFOs, Lake Monsters, Bigfoot and Other Weirdness*. He has written for magazines such as *True West*, *Cinema Retro*, and *Mad Scientist* to name only a few. He is a Past President of the Board of Directors for the Historical Society for Southeast New Mexico.

ALSO AVAILABLE

COWBOYS & SAURIANS
DINOSAURS AND PREHISTORIC BEASTS AS SEEN BY THE PIONEERS

TRUE TALES OF
PREHISTORIC PERIL
FROM THE PIONEER PERIOD!

JOHN LEMAY

If you enjoy *The Real Cowboys and Aliens* series, be sure to check out the *Cowboys & Saurians* series, which examines the possibility of remnant dinosaurs alive and well during America's early days.

This is what Tobias Wayland, of the Singular Fortean Society, had to say about the book:

Cowboys & Saurians: Dinosaurs and Prehistoric Beasts as Seen by the Pioneers, written by John Le May, author of *The Real Cowboys & Aliens: UFO Encounters of the Old West*, and published in September of 2019, is a collection of accounts from the late 19th and early 20th century detailing encounters with seemingly impossible saurians.

LeMay provides a helpful introduction at the beginning of the book to those for whom the idea of remnant dinosaurs might be new, which can be skipped by experienced cryptozoologists already familiar with the subject, before launching directly into the tales of Old West-era monsters with 'The Pterodactyl of Tombstone.' New fans and experienced researchers alike will appreciate his approach to the topic, as LeMay provides a nuanced, well-researched history of the controversial story and its associated photograph—which may or may not exist.

This author isn't afraid to delve into high strangeness, either, and if there are elements thereof existent in an account, LeMay will tell you about them. From the Piasa Bird to the Van Meter Visitor to the Marfa Lights, LeMay offers a wide array of phenomena from off the beaten path. He provides a plethora of sources for each, drawing from historical newspaper accounts and the previous explorations of his fellow cryptozoologists; even peppering the book with the original art and illustrations that went to print, whenever possible.

LeMay doesn't offer a lot of definitive solutions to the mysteries presented in this book, being content to provide the reader with the tools to make their own determination. These stories are wildly entertaining, but hard facts, let alone proof, are difficult to come by, and LeMay is well aware of the struggle intrinsic to the field. To that end, there's no agenda here; he's not trying to sell you a paradigm. The only bill of goods within this book is a batch of intriguing stories, retold with excellent research.

Cowboys & Saurians is a well-researched, open-minded tour of the Old West's most fantastic tales of saurian encounters; sure to appeal to both new seekers and established cryptozoological researchers alike.

www.ingramcontent.com/pod-product-compliance
Lightning Source LLC
Chambersburg PA
CBHW071413070526
44578CB00003B/567